Transform Your Soul

Reflections of a Nurse on Compassion, Healing, and Divine Power

IRENE FULMER, RN

iUniverse LLC
Bloomington

TRANSFORM YOUR SOUL
REFLECTIONS OF A NURSE ON COMPASSION, HEALING, AND DIVINE POWER

iUniverse books may be ordered through booksellers or by contacting:

iUniverse LLC
1663 Liberty Drive
Bloomington, IN 47403
www.iuniverse.com
1-800-Authors (1-800-288-4677)

ISBN: 978-1-4917-1670-0 (sc)
ISBN: 978-1-4917-1669-4 (hc)
ISBN: 978-1-4917-1668-7 (e)

Library of Congress Control Number: 2013921656

Printed in the United States of America.

iUniverse rev. date: 4/07/2014

CONTENTS

FOREWORD

I rene (Victory) Fulmer has offered a victorious invitation into caring and healing and sacred passages for awakening our hearts and humanity. This work embraces the finest of our shared journey into compassion, love, beauty, and life-giving/life-receiving experiences. It is a gift to pause and reflect on the vast array of messages and inner paths this book offers to all who open it.

—Jean Watson, PhD, RN, AHN-BC,FAAN,
Founder/director, Watson Caring Science Institute

Endorsements

I think in this day and present time nurses need "a shot in the arm." That "shot" can be as simple as a patient saying, "Thank you." Sometimes nurses are so involved in caring for the patients they neglect themselves. This book will certainly be the adrenaline needed to help nurses become more attuned to self-care. Irene redefines the vision and direction that nursing should take. She again raises the bar to its rightful place of honor, respect, and true sacrifice. She sounds the alarm to "wake up" our soul and invites us to raise our consciousness and "soar" the uncharted territory of our spirit.

—Ann Tahaney, RN CEN
Former president, Professional Nurses Association
Associate editor, *The Suffolk Nurse*, PNA newsletter
Media chairperson, American Nurses Association, New York

Someone once said, "The very essence of leadership is that you have vision. True leadership cannot blow an uncertain trumpet." If ever there was a need for God-ordained and anointed leadership, it is this present hour. Throughout the world the signs of the times are evident with clear indications that we are transitioning from one age into another. Both the body of Christ and those in the world are longing for someone to clear a path and establish a blueprint to move into the future. That is precisely what the book that you hold in your hand will do.

In her book *Transform Your Soul: Reflections of a Nurse on Compassion, Healing, and Divine Power*, Irene Fulmer meticulously weaves spiritual insight, scientific paradigms, and personal history into this strategic book, which is much needed for these times of great hardship. The lessons they learned and the principles they employed provide valuable tools to forge our future. Such is the case in this book as Irene utilizes great insights from significant spiritual leaders, such as Florence Nightingale, to provide strategy for the days ahead.

This book will inspire and awaken each reader into a place of spiritual understanding. The scriptures describe a great prophet by the name of Daniel who received divine inspiration and was given "insight with understanding." That is what this book will provide to those who diligently apply its truth, and that is why I gladly recommend it.

—Paul Keith Davis, White Dove Ministries

I have known Irene Fulmer for several years as she has frequently attended my supernatural training schools and seminars around the nation. So you can imagine how thrilled I was when she told me that she was inspired to write a book. I've heard many of her healing testimonies and know the great influence that Irene carries within the nursing community, but now her writings are available as a great blessing to a wider audience. Irene Fulmer is being used by God to bring healing to the whole man as she reaches out with the compassion, wisdom, and miracle-working power of Christ. You will be blessed as you read this book and gain insight to *Transform Your Soul*.

—Joshua Mills
Keynote conference speaker and best-selling author,
31 Days to a Miracle Mindset
Vancouver, Canada/Palm Springs, California
www.JoshuaMills.com

ACKNOWLEDGMENTS

To my son, Jeff, and my daughter, Jennifer. You both have been the true treasures of my life. Thank you for your love and encouragement in my journey as a mom, nurse, and writer. Thank you for understanding my insatiable passion to find God. Thank you to my four amazing grandchildren: Alex, Annalise, Hayden, and Anna Marie. I love you all dearly.

To Wade Taylor, my teacher, mentor, and dear friend. Words fail to capture the gratitude I have in my heart for you. Wade went to his eternal reward one year ago at age eighty-seven. He was the founder of Pinecrest Bible Training Center in Salisbury, New York, and its leader for thirty-eight years. He then founded Parousia Ministries, which is based in the Washington, DC, area. Today his teachings continue to be available at www.wadetaylor.org. In 1959, he was taken up to heaven and stood before God's throne. The angels covered him with the powerful glory emanating from the throne. It was there that Wade was commissioned to teach and train those interested in preparing to be a part of God's purposes in the closing of the present age; I was one of those people. Wade believed that our time on earth is a probationary period and that in this time we have been given the opportunity to become overcomers (to come out of the lower nature into the spirit nature) and thereby qualify for the end time purposes of God. He understood that if we are to have a part in the millennium reign of God on the earth, it is essential for us to function in the realm of the spirit apart from human thought processes. Wade said, "Those who truly make a difference in this world are the overcomers, because they bring the substance—the very essence—of God into the world." These are humble ones, who don't try to be more than they are but simply go through the process of preempting the self-life and its natural abilities, which are good—for the greater gain of spirit. It is the *overcomers* who have moved away the stone blocking the soul's ability to function from the deeper core of their beings. The reason is this: it's not about what we are *doing*, but it is very much about what we are *becoming*. (This is from Wade's book, *Unlocking the Mysteries of the Kingdom*.) When there is no self-ambition, no thoughts of *what's in it for me?*—we become the reflection of spirit; it is in this light of God's nature coming through us that we have access to greater authority. Through the process of becoming empty, we become full, making more room for spirit to increase.

That I will cause all those that love me to inherit substance and I will fill their treasures.—Proverbs 8:21 KJV

INTRODUCTION

This book comes out of a deep longing to honor nurses. It comes to esteem every woman or man who has chosen to add "nurse" to the title of their names and to proclaim the profound sacredness of the nursing profession and its myriad forms and manifestations of healing the sick. As an expectant mother waits until her fullness of time comes, so it is with this book; the time has come for its fulfillment. Its sole purpose is to inspire you to the richness of this sacred calling and the transformational power it holds for you. You are the hands that touch and the voice that brings the message of caring to the sick and dying. Your daily labors of love, patience, and hard work have been precious seeds for healing. Remember, you are the key to every kind of healing, for compassion is the true healer within you.

This writing has been in my thoughts and has evolved over a career of almost thirty years in the nursing profession. Many times, I seek solitude to reflect and clarify my thoughts in a quiet place of retreat at the Pinecrest Bible and Retreat Center, where I studied and recently was ordained. It's located in the foothills of the Adirondack Mountains, where nature offers a breathtaking view of majestic mountains and stately landscapes, with many tall trees and flowing streams of water. What I value most is the silence that connects me to God's presence, wisdom, and mystery. It places everything into the right perspective and alignment for me—living primarily from spirit, then from soul, and lastly, from the body.

My curiosity and passion to nurture the patient and the nurses' soul/spirit led to my study of holistic medicine. The New York College of Holistic Medicine on Long Island offers a two-year program in traditional Chinese medicine, with courses that include Chinese herbs, holistic nutrition, Amma massage therapy, and pulse diagnosis. Their theory of wholism gave more meaning and depth to the caring process for the sick. Caring is not only for the body but for the soul and spirit, honoring the whole person—not just the symptoms and disease.

Over the past decade, new doors of opportunity have opened to practice the dimensions of spirit reality, the metaphysical realm of energy, and awareness of the Creator's presence. Using intentionality at the patient's bedside changed the atmosphere and brought about a metaphysical phenomenon for the patient to experience. The positive effects it has on the patients has been inspiring and rewarding. A "Caring for the Nurse" educational series was introduced for the nurses at North Shore Hospital's Syosset and Plainview sites, where holistic concepts were taught and demonstrated. The series offered nurses guided imagery/meditation, Amma massage therapy, holistic nutrition, and exercise classes including tai chi, dance, and yoga. Holistic concepts of caring have truly complemented the western medical model of health care at both hospitals. As coordinator of the complementary integrative medicine for the past twelve years, I have incorporated Florence Nightingale's holistic perspectives on caring for the whole person and disease prevention. In this holistic environment other opportunities have opened for formal research studies using holistic therapies with cancer patients and bariatric patients. Through the many years of nursing new doors of opportunities have opened through travel to Germany, Italy, France, and Hawaii, as well as opportunities for humanitarian outreach in Africa, Israel, and Palestine.

Florence Nightingale and Jean Watson were inspirations in formulating and validating my ideas and beliefs. Now over a hundred years old, nursing has evolved through the decades as one of the pillars of healthcare. Nursing must now clarify its heritage and redefine itself—or be in danger of losing its soul, its meaning, and its relevance in today's world. I am committed to recovering the soul of nursing. Nursing must reclaim and reintegrate the original tenets of Nightingale. They are timeless and noble ideals and the direction for nursing to move toward. Nightingale acknowledged that nursing was a calling and a spiritual practice. I am certain that nursing is a reflection of the divine; its calling is to mirror caring and compassion to the sick. My anguish is watching nursing struggle; it carries the pain and suffering of society but is tied to an old, depleted medical-clinical model view of humans—not knowing its own power, purpose, and destiny. I have committed myself to the healing of nurses and mankind.

In her book, *Human Caring Science: A Theory of Nursing*, Watson indicates that this human care role is now being threatened by increased medical, technological, economic, bureaucratic, and managerial institutional constraints and that nursing is going through dramatic, chaotic, and unprecedented change. She warns of the human threats from biotechnology, scientific engineering, fragmented treatment, economic mandates, and depersonalization; these continue to spread throughout our health-care delivery system, so she urges us to increase and radiate the human caring philosophy, knowledge, and practices. Watson believes the nursing profession has an ethical and social responsibility to both individuals and society to sustain human caring when it is threatened and to be the guardian of human caring—serving as a vanguard of society's human caring needs. She warns that if nursing does not fulfill its societal mandate for sustaining human caring and preserving human dignity and humanness in self, systems, and society—it will not be carrying out its covenant to society and its very reason for existence as a profession.

In *Human Caring Science*, Watson proposes a theory of human caring science that brings the framework and concepts of the soul and spirit back into nursing.

Watson's theory defines a quality of human consciousness that cannot be equated with the physical body—but rather *transcends* it. Nursing must now address this human caring concept of love in its caring model and make the ethical, philosophical, and moral values of nursing more explicit at the theoretical level. In *Human Caring Science*, Watson asks: "What lens do we hold toward knowing/being/doing in relation to human caring and humanity, health-illness, healing, suffering, living, dying, and all the vicissitudes of life that nurses experience every day?" Watson changed the title of her original book from *Nursing: Human Science and Human Care* to *Human Caring Science: A Theory of Nursing* for her second edition. In the preface of the new edition, she writes, "the words 'human care' in the original book have been changed to 'human caring' to convey a deeper human-to-human involvement and connection one to another, which goes beyond the more concrete notion of what can be implied with the term *human care*. That is, one can offer human care without caring for or caring about the other person, limiting the authentic ethical relational caring processes contained within this theory and unitary views of person and universe."

Nursing's role in human caring must begin with *self* and then it will radiate out to others. I write this for nurses first and then for nursing's future emergence into her rightful place—a right order relating to that which is greater than us all, a returning to love and to the divine order. An existential paradigm shift is needed. It's the only way to sustain us—to sustain humanity. The word *theory* in Greek means *theos*, meaning God and *oros*, which means "to perceive" or "to see." I invite nurses to become visionary leaders, to recreate and reshape a new emerging consciousness of spirit into new models for nursing practice. Nursing needs an authentic caring-healing model of care.

One of the most eloquent quotes is from Pierre Teilhard de Chardin's book, *The Phenomenon of Man*, which defines the direction mankind, is moving:

> What we are up against is the heavy swell of an unknown sea which we are just entering from behind the cape that protected us. What is troubling us intellectually, politically, and even spiritually is something quite simple . . . "We have only just cast off the last moorings which held us to the Neolithic age" . . . We are, at this very moment, passing through a change of age. Beneath a change of age lies a change of thought. Where are we to look for it, where are we to situate this renovating and subtle alteration which, without appreciably changing our bodies, has made new creatures of us? In one place and one only—in a new intuition involving a total change in the physiognomy of the universe in which we move—in other words, in an awakening. (Teilhard de Chardin 1959, 214–215)

We are moving into a new age and mankind is awakening to its new birth.

This book is a compass to help you chart your course into the uncharted waters of your own awakening and to help you discover your authentic soul.

Chapter 2 outlines how to move nursing forward from the traditional western medical model and thought process to a new emerging transcendence of God consciousness in nursing and health care. Here, Nightingale and Watson will expand your view of the theoretical premises of the human caring act and will also expand on the following concept: to the extent that genuineness, sincerity, empathy, and warmth are conveyed by the nurse—the same depth of transcendence and transpersonal union will be achieved at the bedside for the nurse and the patient. It will benefit those who are awakening spiritually and who want to transform their spirituality into nursing practice.

Chapter 3 shows you how to awaken to the transcendence of the human thought processes and how to live above all thought. Experience the new mind, the transcendence into a higher consciousness of your spirit-self. The simplest of souls can touch God, live in the very presence of God and know his power. Human intellect is not an assistant to knowing God; rather, it is a deterrent. You will learn how to overcome the obstructive knowledge and pride that has been developed in your own soul/mind. Through this process of casting off old thought patterns, you will become childlike enough to believe God like a little child does. Discover how to become victorious over what you say and how to free you from the snare of negative words. Gain insight into the consequences of your words and intentions. Discover how words can change the atmosphere around you. Learn how words can affect your health.

Chapter 5 acknowledges and defines—in a practical way—how you can experience quantum concepts, intentionality, nonphysical locality, and God consciousness. It will open a path of light and illumination for you to begin to live in the power of your spirit-self. Discover the manifest presence and experience your union with the divine. Expect some positive changes and benefits to occur. Learn how to gain inner strength and confidence, regardless of outer conditions and circumstances. Instead of circumstances controlling you, *you* are controlling the circumstances. Experience a new freedom governed by spirit, not by emotions or fears. Receive new confidence in the overshadowing of God.

Chapter 8 will inspire and awaken your own authentic soul and spirituality. Launch into the deep waters of spirit; be led into great silence. Experience your authentic self, your soul, and your union with the divine. Discover why you don't believe and why doubt happens. Doubt happens when a person's spiritual connection with God has deteriorated. The elements that come from heaven are not there. The light and radiance from God's heart is not reaching them. Learn how to pray. Learn how to transcend time and space.

Experience the power of the age to come. Experience the bliss of the overshadowing presence of God. Learn the "three keys of caring," a formula you can bring to the patient's bedside. Daily use will make it a part of your nursing practice. You can create the atmosphere of heaven.

> *All transformation begins and ends with self. It is here, with self, that we are required to expand our reality and consciousness.*—Lewis Mumford

Santa Filomena— Florence Nightingale

When'er a noble deed is wrought,
When'er spoken a noble thought,
Our hearts, in glad surprise,
To higher levels rise.

The tidal wave of deeper souls
Into our inmost being rolls,
And lifts us unawares
Out of all meaner cares.

Honor to those whose words or deeds
Thus help us in our daily needs,
And by their overflow
Raise us from what is low!

Thus thought I, as by night I read
of the great army of the dead,
the trenches cold and damp,
the starved and frozen camp,

The wounded from the battle-plain,
In dreary hospitals of pain,
The cheerless corridors,
The cold and stony floors,

Lo, in that house of misery
A lady with a lamp I see
Pass through the glimmering gloom,
And flit from room to room.

And slow, as in a dream of bliss,
The speechless sufferer turns to kiss
Her shadow, as it falls
Upon the darkening walls.

As if a door in heaven should be
Opened, and then closed suddenly,
The vision came and went,
The light shone was spent.

On England's annals, through the long
Hereafter of her speech and song,
That light its rays shall cast
From portals of the past.

A lady with a lamp shall stand
In the great history of the land,
A noble type of good,
Heroic womanhood.

Nor even shall be wanting here
The palm, the lily, and the spear,
The symbols that of yore
Saint Filomena bore.

MISS NIGHTINGALE, IN THE HOSPITAL, AT SCUTARI.—(SEE PRECEDING PAGE.)

TRANSFORMED

CHAPTER 1

MY CALL TO NURSING

Many years ago, when I was a stay-at-home mom raising my children, I had a recurring vision. I saw Jesus walking down the corridor of a hospital. I watched him go from room to room. He wore a white robe with a tie around the waist and sandals on his feet. He had a lowly and humble appearance. Although the vision had a profound effect on me, I wasn't sure what to do with it. After a while, I decided to do volunteer work at a nearby hospital. Sometimes I fed the patients or gave them a drink of water; whichever way I helped them, I experienced a great compassion come over me and could feel spiritual energy flowing to them when I was with them. One day while I was going to a patient's room, I noticed a picture on the wall in the hallway. The words jumped right out at me; it almost seemed as though they went into me. The words were: *The greatest journey ever is the journey inward.* I guessed it was there for a surgeon to ponder over, yet I knew the message was clearly for me. Eventually, I understood that I was being called to become a nurse—yet I had no desire to be one. In fact, I didn't even like going to hospitals; the awful smell and the sounds of suffering made me uncomfortable. Worst of all, seeing blood caused me to faint. I dismissed the call to be a nurse, and since I had a passion for English literature and poetry, I thought I would eventually teach

1

those subjects. In times of solitude, however, the stirring in my soul deeply affected me. Was I being asked to do something I wasn't comfortable doing? Somehow, I knew I had to accept the offer.

Before long, I found myself in an anatomy and physiology class dissecting a cat. My lab partner, Elaine, had a pet cat and couldn't bear the task. She covered the cat's head with a brown bag and I became the designated dissector. This experience left me unable to eat meat for several months. Soon I learned that blood was the "life" of the body and somehow got over fainting when I saw it. One day, the student nurse standing next to me fainted during a surgical procedure we had to observe in the operating room. I was grateful to still be standing that day. There were many tests to pass and many bumps to jump in the road. It wasn't long before I discovered I couldn't cope with sick children, and when we did the geriatric rotation, I realized I had a fear of the elderly. During the psych rotation, I discovered I feared the mentally ill, too. I began to wonder, *did I hear you clearly, God?* It was all so uncomfortable, but I faced my fears, dealt with them, and dismissed them one by one. I was discovering that my journey inward was becoming a journey of healing for myself. After graduation I got my first job in cardiac nursing at St. Francis Hospital in New York. It was unheard of that a new graduate with no experience would be hired, but with the severe nursing shortage in the 1980s, hospitals hired many new grads. Since I had strong compassion for the mentally ill, within a few years I began working with them. Psychiatry was comfortable and exciting. I easily and quite naturally excelled in the field. I had a passion for creative group therapy, interactive group therapy, and individual therapy. I studied for three years with Dr. Jay Earley and two years with Dr. Michael Beck. Using interventional guided imagery groups for the drug and alcohol populations brought remarkable outcomes. Aromatherapy groups had amazing results with depressed and anxious patients. I had found my niche.

I marvel at the faithfulness of God. Over time, I learned that the things he valued in me were very different from what *I* thought was important. God's desire is for our souls to be healed and transformed. His compassion is always toward us. He is a master potter and we are the clay—he molds and shapes us into what he fashions us to become, if we let him. I'm glad I said "yes."

When my journey in psychiatry (my schooling of the spirit) was finished and I had completed many tests and obstacles, I was promoted—not only on a spiritual level but also with a new job. After approval came from the medical board at North Shore Syosset and Plainview hospitals, I started my new position as a holistic nurse coordinator of complementary integrative medicine. That very day, I had the opportunity to help a doctor's wife. She had lymphoma and permanent nerve damage to both of her hands. When we met, the door practically knocked her over because she was so weak, but something miraculous started to happen when I placed my hands on her. A virtuous substance began to flow out from my hands into her body. I was dazzled by it and so was she. Each meeting with her brought the same miraculous flow of divine substance through my hands and into her body. On our eighth visit, the permanent nerve damage to her hands was gone. Not only could she move all her fingers again, but her pain was completely gone. God is in us all if we make room for him, and if we give him preeminence, we will see miracles.

I have finally come to understand the vision that started my journey. God is a healer in me.

CHAPTER 2

AN OVERVIEW: FROM NIGHTINGALE TO WATSON

These two visionary pioneers changed nursing forever. Their vision transformed nursing and continues to reform nursing around the world—challenging us into the twenty-first century. Their revelatory light reflects the sacred . . . the heart of nursing . . . the heart of God, caring for the sick and the dying.

Nightingale's life demonstrated a profound, heavenly calling to alleviate human pain and suffering in this world. She believed that her life could be in harmony with God and that spirituality was the path to attain it ["spirituality: an ontologically driven impulse toward union or relationship with God or ultimate transcendent reality" (Hodge 2001).

Longfellow suggests in his poem that Nightingale was divinely inspired. The line "as if a door from heaven should be opened" can be interpreted as illuminating rays of divine light shining into her life and the work that followed. Her lamp became a symbol, first of her exemplary caring during a deeply troubled period and then of the illumination her insights have brought later in her career. Her devotion to her calling was a gift from God. Her sole ambition was to raise the consciousness of nursing and nineteenth century health care.

Florence Nightingale was born in Florence, Italy on May 12, 1820, while her parents were on an extended European tour. They were a wealthy English family, active in politics. Her father—a gentle, understanding man—was educated at Cambridge and educated Florence at home. She became fluent in French, German, Italian, Latin, and Greek. After a serious seven-year courtship with a popular politician and poet, she broke off the relationship and refused his marriage proposal. She chose to remain single to better serve God and mankind. She sought out the Kaiserswerth Institute in Dusseldorf, Germany, and in 1850 she visited it for two weeks of observation followed by a month of rudimentary training. Nightingale was one of the most knowledgeable people in Europe on the subjects of hospitals, hospital construction, and health care. She acquired this knowledge before the age of thirty and with no formal training—only the information she had collected through her well-placed friends, many of whom were politicians and physicians. Her epic leadership at the Barrack Hospital in Scutari, Turkey during the Crimean War (1854–1856) exemplifies how she built the powerful and political ties that led to the resolution of grievous problems in army structure and organization. In 1860, she founded a training school for nurses in London, the first modern secular school of nursing (Dossey 2005).

In her day, Nightingale was a revolutionary, overflowing with ideas that seemed too altruistic to be realistic. Today, although we have an entirely different health-care delivery system, her values and ideas remain an invaluable cornerstone of the nursing profession. She endorsed nursing as a work of service to others that would restore and promote a healthy body, mind/soul, and spirit, and that would prevent disease.

It is not very well known that Nightingale was also a practical mystic and spiritual caregiver. Barbara Dossey's comprehensive history, *Florence Nightingale: Mystic, Visionary, Healer*, includes the following—written by Nightingale about her attraction to nursing: "The first idea I can recollect when I was a child was a desire to nurse the sick. My day dreams were all of hospitals and I visited them whenever I could . . . I thought God had called me to serve Him in this way" (2009).

Nightingale understood that her call to nursing was essentially a spiritual practice. When she was seventeen—and two other times in her life—she heard God's voice. The flame in her lamp at Scutari Hospital in Turkey was famous. She felt a divine spark had been ignited within her. She vigilantly followed her sense of divine guidance as she faced her own dark times, including years of disapproval from her mother for becoming a nurse and decades of chronic illness and pain.

She allowed the spark to shed light on the health issues of her time, as she advocated for individual and public health care, as well as for human rights and social justice. Her focus was on people, their health, and proactive ways to stay healthy—rather than simply treating disease. One of the major distinctions she made in her lifetime was between *nursing for illness* and *nursing for health*. Her goal for "sick-nursing" was always to assist the suffering so that they lived through the "natural" illness process. Her goals for "health-nursing" were to strengthen the conditions supporting health and wellness and to nurture those conditions—those positive health determinants meant to prevent disease.

In 1872, Nightingale began her book on practical mysticism, *Notes from Devotional Authors of the Middle Ages*. In her writings, Nightingale defines *mysticism* as follows: "to dwell on the unseen, to withdraw ourselves from the things of sense into communion with God" (McDonald 2002). Nightingale believed that healing was the essence of nursing, and she understood it needed to incorporate a holistic approach to achieve balance and integration. (*Holistic healing* is the bringing together of body, mind, and spirit.) She explored the complex nature of healing from many viewpoints. Her source of strength and guidance for her work was service to God and others. Nightingale raised questions about what it means to be human, to be cared for, and to be healed. She expanded her worldview by studying philosophy and by exploring the nature of knowledge and ways of knowing reality. She included spirituality as a driving force in healing; for her, it was the life principle in humans. It was the thinking, motivating, and feeling part of the human experience that was important in healing; she believed it involved a sense of connectedness with a power that is greater, wiser, and more majestic than the individual self. She gained insight into the word *spirit* as derived from the Latin *spiritus,* meaning "breath" or "air." Spirituality gave meaning to her life; she believed it to be the unifying force connecting the self with others, nature, and God—which is the essence of all of life.

Nightingale believed that medicine was not a curative process; she understood that while it removed obstructions to the cure, only *nature* could cure the body. Her goal was to "place the patient in the best possible position for nature to heal" (Nightingale 1859), an approach that still finds its place in the twenty-first century at the patient's bedside. She dramatically changed health care with a simple yet profound discovery: *hand washing* could control the spread of disease and infection. Although over 150 years have passed since this discovery, hand washing is still the number one method used to fight infection and combat disease.

Nightingale's life and work demonstrates *integral nursing,* an integral approach with "wholeness as its goal—dynamic, interdependent, open, fluid, and continuously interacting with changing variables that can lead to greater complexity and order" (Dossey 2005). Nightingale is also an example of a powerful trans-disciplinarian. She was always analyzing, communicating, exchanging, surveying, involving, synthesizing, investigating, interviewing, mentoring, developing, creating, researching, and teaching. She listened to others and created new schemes for what was possible. Transdisciplinary dialogues are transformative and visionary, facilitating and leading to the creation of total healing environments.

During her lifetime, Nightingale authored over a hundred books and documents. Her letters—numbering more than ten thousand—are in the British Library in London. Nightingale wrote the following letter on May 6, 1881, in London:

To the Nurses and Probationers of St. Thomas' Hospital

> My very dear friends,
> Now once more "God speed" to you all; my very best greetings and thanks to you all: to our beginners good courage, to our dear old workers peace, fresh courage too, perseverance: for to persevere to the end is as difficult and needs better energy than to begin new work. To be a good Nurse one must be a good woman: here we shall all agree. It is the old, old story. But some of us are new to the start. What is it to be "like a woman"?—"a very woman" is sometimes said as a word of contempt: sometimes as a word of tender admiration. What makes a good woman is the better or higher or holier nature: quietness—gentleness—patience—endurance—forbearance—forbearance with her patients—her fellow workers—her superiors—her equals. We need to remember that we come to learn, to be taught. Hence we come to obey. No one ever was able to govern who was not able to obey. No one ever was able to teach who was not able to learn. The best scholars make the best teachers—those who obey best, the best rulers. (Dossey 2005)

Nightingale's ambition was to integrate spiritual principles into her work ethic in order to bring about reform. She said, "Nursing is an art, and, if it is to be made an art, requires as exclusive a devotion, as hard a preparation, as any painter's or sculptor's work; for what is having to do with dead canvas or cold marble, compared with having to do with the living body- the temple of God's spirit? It is one of the fine Arts; I had almost said, the finest of the Fine Arts" (1868) She discovered that aligning with spiritual laws gave her access to spiritual authority and was able to bring that into her own life and work. She understood the importance of walking in humility, which enabled her to cultivate an attitude of putting others over oneself. She acknowledged her oneness with humanity and the value each soul to its creator. Nightingale was graced with a universal compassion that showed no partiality. She believed true leadership should serve others. As she aligned herself with these principles, her life began to flourish. By the end of her life, Nightingale had training schools in twenty countries; the United States alone had a thousand schools.

In 1989 a museum was made in her honor at St. Thomas' Hospital in London on the south bank of the River Thames. It displays a unique collection of her personal possessions, artifacts connected with her nursing and humanitarian work in the Crimean War, and nursing material from the Nightingale Training School from its inception in 1860. On Saturday, August 13, 1910, at age ninety, Nightingale fell asleep at noon and never awoke again (Dossey 2005).

Reigniting the Flame of Their Legacy

A century later, Jean Watson reignited the mission that Florence Nightingale had begun. Watson picked up the baton—moving the reformation forward—and Nightingale was reborn. Jean Watson's depth, passion, and pioneering spirit have reflected a timeless zeal that has reawakened nurses to their mission. Watson also believes it is important to revere the wonders and mysteries of life and acknowledge life's spiritual dimension; she believes in the human care process to produce growth and change. She worked to help nurses gain more self-knowledge, self-control, and readiness for self-healing.

Watson's caring model states that the act of caring for the patient must have a moral dimension, with a spiritual connection between the patient and the nurse characterized by cooperation and connectedness (Watson's *Human Science and Human Care* 1999). Underlying her belief system is a revaluing of human care in nursing theory and practice. She believes that every human being deserves respect and strongly reasserted nursing's obligation to preserve the dignity and worth of each person. In her model of the dynamic nature of human caring transaction, Watson depicts the nurse-patient as individual selves—each enveloped by a phenomenal field of subjective meanings. The two people in a caring transaction are both in the process of being and becoming. The moment of coming together in an actual caring occasion presents the opportunity for each person to learn from the other how to be human. Watson has implied more than a mere merging of experiences; she has suggested there is a spiritual union of souls. This kind of caring interaction with another "self" stands as a moral imperative for any nurse committed to the art of transpersonal care (Watson 1999).

Watson uses the notion of a caring field to convey the quantum concept of waves radiating from each person and becoming part of a new field of possibility, all within a caring moment, affected by one's consciousness and intentionality (Watson 1999).

Watson defines *transpersonal care* as the "capacity of one human being to receive another human being's expression of feeling and to experience those feelings for oneself" (Watson 1985, 67). She believes that transpersonal care is much more than a scripted therapeutic response; it is a moral duty that arises from within the nurse. Watson identifies nursing as both an art and a science. She believes that the closer nurse caring approximates the moral ideal of transpersonal caring—the empathy and warmth of the nurse—the better the recipient will assimilate perceived self with the self "as is." Watson admits to freely drawing upon the theoretical work of psychotherapist and humanistic researcher, Carl Rogers (Rogers 1990).

Watson's idealism is expressed in such a way that nurses can use their own personalities and unique styles to implement a number of existential concepts. She postulates that being heard and understood by another person is a life-changing experience; this honors the human quest for wholeness and fosters self-help. Her ambition is to establish a metaphysical foundation for nursing's imperative to care. Her theory of focusing beyond the *cure* factor to the *care* factor—and her goals to include mental and spiritual growth for oneself and for other nurses—has led to her global recognition.

The Challenge and Opportunity for Nursing

As a pioneer in nursing's evolution, Jean Watson believed that the challenge for nursing was to redefine itself from the nursing medical paradigm and to reaffirm a nursing postmodern paradigm—reclaiming its sacred feminine caring-healing archetype. Watson says that such a radical rethinking of nursing is so necessary at this point in human and nursing history. It requires a shift from the modern, industrial, patriarchal framework to postmodern caring-healing practices. Such a shift will take nursing into the twenty-first century with the rights, autonomy, potential, and power to transform itself; nursing will be a cocreator with like-minded others to go beyond the Western medical mind-set and become something new and different. Watson says that this "something new" is already inscribed in the textual core of nursing—it is its soul.

As we move into the twenty-first century, the nursing profession has to examine its identity, its boundaries, its maturity, its paradigms, its education, and its practice models. In this present year of 2014 nursing stands between two worlds and times. Many issues still linger unresolved and are caught between modern and postmodern dilemmas. Watson says that nursing, along with all other professions and disciplines, is witnessing the simultaneous peak and erosion of the Western culture cosmology.

In her book, *Human Caring Science*, Watson writes: "Nursing has been unclear about its direction and standing, in that the pressures from objective views of science, methodological dictates, medical preoccupation, and clinical physical foci and restrictions have often taken nursing off course from its own development and clarity."

The concepts involved in nursing caring science are not just clinical, biophysical phenomenon, but also ethical, philosophical, spiritual, and metaphysical phenomenon. Watson said, *"These have to be honored and acknowledged in nursing practice"*

(Lecture, March 2013).

Can nursing become one that is more consistent with nursing's values and philosophy? In order to transform and redefine itself, nursing must face some new truths about its power and possibilities; one solution is a new lens for seeing. Some say the repression of the feminine in our world is a pathology that inhibits our growth. Beginning with Nightingale, nursing continues to embrace a deep ethical, philosophical, and moral covenant with society. Watson says this orientation and deep commitment to humanity and caring phenomena have not always been understood by the outer world of medicine and conventional science (Watson 2012).

Today, nursing is at a crossroads. The difficulties are many, and we can struggle along as nurses have before—or we can stop to reconsider and focus on what nursing can become. Nightingale's generation needed *her*; our present world needs *nursing*. Like Nightingale and Watson, nurses can become global visionaries for the health of humanity.

Joseph Campbell was a mythologist, writer, and lecturer, best known for his comparative mythology. In 1972 he wrote, "We are a culture and medical system that has lost its center because we have cut ourselves off from our meanings, symbols, and myths. We have lost the sacred and the soul." Campbell believed that as a culture we devalue what we have forgotten. The sacred feminine archetype principle has been used across time as a road to the sacred, and without it we cut ourselves off from the life source. Nursing, medicine, and all humanity must rediscover its own soul—or it will end up destroying itself (Campbell 1972).

"As we examine our truth of Belonging-Being-Knowing and Doing-Caring-Healing work in the world, how can we any longer bear to sustain and perpetuate an empty, hollow model?" Watson (2011)

Watson expresses the idea that society needs the caring professions and nursing in particular to help restore humanity and nourish the human heart and soul in an age of technology, scientism, loneliness, rapid change, and stresses, an age without moral or ethical wisdom as to how to serve humanity. Watson acknowledges that this particular theory of nursing is metaphysical in that it incorporates the concept of the soul and transcendence. Although the human soul is nothing new, it is, however, unusual to include it in a theory. Her bold attempt to acknowledge and incorporate a concept of the soul in a nursing theory is a reflection of an alternative position that nursing is now free to take. Watson says this new concept breaks away from the traditional medical science model. She believes the evolution of the history and philosophy of science now allows focus on metaphysical views that were unacceptable at an earlier point in time (Watson 2012).

Watson's beliefs and values about human life provide a foundation for her theory of nursing, and they also influence the subject matter of the theory. She has outlined a basic premise of which there are seven. Here are two of them:

> A person's consciousness and emotions are windows to the soul. Nursing care can be and is physical, procedural, objective, and factual, but at the highest level of nursing the nurses human caring responses, the human caring connections and the nurses' presence in the relationship transcend the physical and material world, bound in time and space, and make contact with the person's spirit-filled subjective world as the route to the inner self and the higher sense of self. So we open to an evolving consciousness throughout the lifetime to evolve toward a higher consciousness. We may pose the question, "What is the highest level of consciousness? Is it not love? Are we

not evolving to become more loving and therefore more godly as God is love?"

Here is yet another description of Watson's basic premise:

> People need each other in a caring, loving way. Love and caring are two universal givens. To paraphrase Teilhard de Chardin, love (and care) are the most universal, the most tremendous, and the most mysterious of cosmic forces. It is the primal and universal psychic energy (1967). These needs are often overlooked, because even though we know we need one another in a loving and caring way, we do not behave well toward each other. If our humanness is to survive, we need to become more loving, caring, and moral to nourish our humanity, advance as a civilization, and live together. As a beginning we need to impose our own will to love, care, and be moral upon our own behavior, not on others' behavior. We need to love, respect, and care for ourselves and treat ourselves with dignity before we can respect, love, and care for others and treat them with dignity. (Watson 2005)

In Watson's human caring science she defines the value inherent in this (nursing) work is associated with deep respect and openness for the wonders, mysteries, and even miracles of life and the power for humans to change. In the views of Teilhard de Chardin one wants to evolve toward the omega point, to become more godly, more holy, more divine, more in line with one's spiritual destiny, dignity, and the soul's code.

I had the privilege of meeting Jean Watson in March 2013 at a lecture she gave on her "Ten Caritas Processes" at Molloy College on Long Island. She said, "You can't remain in the old paradigm; you must be transformed. Heart-centered loving kindness changes the whole environmental field; we are the ultimate environment. We must do things to help change it. Touch another person, be open to existential unknowns—allow for mystery and miracles." These are just a few of the powerful statements she made. I had the wonderful opportunity of meeting with her after her lecture. What touched me most was her loving and caring presence. I felt like we had known each other forever. She radiated the love of God. I could feel her genuineness and compassion toward me and her enthusiastic interest in my book. She has certainly evolved from knowing and doing to *becoming*. She *is* her message.

Throughout the North Shore-LIJ Health System at Syosset and Plainview where I work, Nursing's path is illuminated by the seminal work of Florence Nightingale and practice is undergirded by Jean Watson's Theory of Human Caring. 'Caring' is also a core value of the organization' 'Collaborative Care Model'. In 2004, the Institute for Nursing was created. The institute established a professional practice environment to advance the art and science of nursing through the melding of nursing education, research, and practice. As nursing practice has evolved, it is becoming more transparent and is undergoing a great transformational change. Nursing has a new focus, with nobler ideals on caring, inclusion, respect, attitude, value, and the concept of honoring self and others. The outcomes have led to a letting go of the self-focused ego, as well as declines in abuse of power and unhealthy competitiveness between interdisciplinary hospital staff. New attitudes of teamwork and camaraderie are emerging, creating a more nurturing, healing environment. The director of the institute, Maureen White, said that the support from Michael Dowling (president and CEO) and from the board of trustees created an environment that allowed her to pursue endless possibilities for advancing nursing practice (Boyd 2013).

Nursing's Aging Population

Many nurses in the health-care industry are from the baby boomer generation and have already retired or are getting ready to retire. I am one of them. These retirement years should be some of the best years. Retirement offers the greatest commodity—time. Extra time is an invaluable asset. Retirement is an exciting marker of reaping the rewards of life's toils and labors. Now there is time to do things we never had time for before. Since time is so valuable, full retirement—or even partial retirement—is a true blessing. Those nearing retirement can be optimistic, carefree, and spontaneous with the future. Make plans to enjoy life in the myriad ways we desire to. When he was seventy-eight, General Douglas MacArthur declared, "Nobody grows old by merely living a number of years. People grow old by deserting their ideals. Years may wrinkle the skin, but to give up interest wrinkles the soul." Although Winston Churchill was worthy of retirement at age seventy-nine, instead he picked up a pen and won the Nobel Prize in literature. Time slips quickly by; days pass into months, and months pass into years, and what we came to do must be done while there is time. Age should not be an enemy; age is only a mile marker on our journey. The years after retirement should be some of the best years of our lives. All the previous years of growth, preparation, and development refine us into the "best vintage wine." Robert Browning said it well in a poem he wrote in 1864: "Grow old along with me! The best is yet to be, the last of life, for which the first was made" (Louchs and Stauffer 2007). After Michelangelo died, someone found a note in his studio that he had written to his apprentice. In the handwriting of his old age, the great artist wrote, "Draw Antonio, draw, and do not waste time" (Lucado 1999).

CHAPTER 3

THE POWER OF WORDS

The words of the wise bring healing.
—Proverbs 12:18, Webster's Bible Translation, 2007

Humans are very vocal creatures and are not always aware of the consequences of our words. Scientists tell us that our speech directly affects our nervous system and that even the atoms and molecules in our bodies respond to what we think and say. Psychologists and linguistics have been studying the effects of words for many years. They say that our words begin in the mind as pictures, a fraction of a second before we speak them. They tell us that the world around us is held together by our thoughts, words, desires, and feelings. The physical world exists as possibilities, and our words and feelings actually form our destiny.

The scriptures tell us that the physical world was made by unseen powers. Faith (which one believes) is "the substance of things hoped for, the evidence of things not seen" (Hebrews 11:1 KJV) on a quantum level. Everything is made up of atoms, which are frequencies of energy. These frequencies of energy are the voice of the creator causing all things to be. Our words and desires emanate from us as a form of light and color. This information flows from our future possibilities—waiting for us to see, to observe.

Scientists studying an electron particle in a state of flux noticed that the particle changed when observed. Under certain conditions, these subatomic structures also take on the properties of invisible waves. Although we don't always know the immediate effects of our words when we abuse them, they affect everything around us. Everything we say has a direct influence on the unseen realm. Our words are the interacting catalyst between two realms—the natural and the spiritual—and we forget that there are consequences to what we say. Faith is an unseen substance on a quantum level and is an unseen energy that forms matter into what is spoken and believed. As we believe, we will become.

> *Pleasant words are like honey, they are sweet to the spirit and bring healing to the body.*—Proverbs 16:24 NIRV

Words Have Consequences

> *Death and life are in the power of the tongue.*
> —Proverbs 18:21 KJV

The Greek word for word is *logos*. Philosophers and theologians say it is a principle originating in classical Greek thought, referring to a universal, divine reason—immanent in nature yet transcending all oppositions and imperfections in the cosmos and in humanity. It is an eternal and unchanging truth, present from the time of creation and available to every individual who seeks it. This unifying and liberating revelatory force reconciles the human with the divine and manifests in the world as an act of God's love—in the form of the Word. Traditionally, *logos* means word, thought, principle, or speech. It has two main distinctions. The first deals with human reason or the rationality of the human mind, which seeks to attain universal understanding and harmony. The second has to do with universal intelligence—or the universal ruling force governing and revealing the divine through the cosmos to mankind. In the New Testament, the Word of God in John 1:1 shows God's desire and ability to speak to humans. "The Word became flesh" (KJV) points to the possibility of union between the human and the divine. It acts as a bridge between the human's inner spiritual need and the answer recorded through the message of the Word. According to the German-American philosopher and theologian Paul Tillich, "He who sacrifices the Logos principle sacrifices the idea of a living God." In other words, without an understanding of God's love, will, and power as a living and active force in the world—through the logos God and through the participation in the logos with our reason—the message becomes a lifeless and inconsequential set of doctrines which can be accepted or rejected without bearing on one's life. (pbs.org/faithandreason/thegloss/logos-bodyhtml)

Words also have an implied meaning based on the speaker. For instance, if the president of a country makes a speech, the office itself will allow his words to carry more weight than if he were an ordinary citizen saying the same thing. The implication of this principle is that words not only convey meaning, but also they convey the personality and authority of the speaker. Doctors carry authority when they make a diagnosis. Since our words come from within us, they reveal the very intent of our thinking. A double-minded person is one who speaks out one thought but reserves another opinion as well. This can weaken what the person says and cause confusion, leading to instability—because the speaker compromises what is true. Sometimes those with the least authority speak the loudest because of their insecurity. When someone has authority, however, his or her words have the power to influence others positively or negatively, depending on the words they choose and their intent.

Psychologists and philosophers are just starting to understand what has been known for thousands of years. In the scriptures, James 3 tells us that we stumble in many ways and if anyone does not stumble in what he says, he is a perfect man who is able to bridle his whole body (AV). This truth helps us realize that words have consequences. We often say things in anger that we later regret.

Our emotions can have more control over our words than our logic. Sometimes our words are motivated by our insecurity and the need to control a situation. Negative-minded individuals can influence and test our convictions, and we may find our words becoming more negative. Conversely, being with positive individuals can change or renew our thoughts and perspective in a positive way. Many accomplished individuals credit their mentors for their inspiration and success.

Just as important as the words we choose is the *spirit* from which they are spoken. We have the power to bless and curse, and we can create an environment of healing or confusion. Sometimes our body language speaks for us. On a deeper level, the goodness in us doesn't need words to communicate. It communicates through the vibrations of what we have become; this kind of silence can speak louder than words. We can create protected places in our homes and our cars by speaking blessings with our words.

In the sacred writings, the apostle James goes on to say that if someone is so disciplined that they are able to control their speech, they are considered mature or fully tested. He says the way to control our bodies and to avoid its misuse is to control our words. He compares the proper control of the tongue to the control of a horse's bridle. With a small amount of pressure to its mouth, a well-trained horse either starts, stops, or changes direction. The part of the small bridle doing the work is not easily visible, but it can dramatically affect the horse's behavior. Our words have great consequences when spoken. James uses the analogy of a ship's rudder to describe the tongue. It is not the set of the sail or the wind that ultimately determines where we end up in life; it is the tiny rudder, our tongue. James is saying that it is our tongues that control our lives and determine our direction, just as a rudder controls a ship. Most people do not realize the power of their words in determining the outcomes of their lives and whether they will fulfill their destiny or not. We need to understand that our words are creative because we carry a likeness of the Creator—the power to create. Whatever controls our words will also control us. The intent of our words creates a blessing or a curse. Every word, action, and past event has been recorded and stored in matter, because all matter has memory. Our lives will either be lived as a directionless and undisciplined horse, or if we use our words wisely and with discipline, they will direct life's course in a positive direction. What we speak moves us in one direction or another; we need to ask ourselves, "Which way am I going?"

> *I call heaven and earth to record this day against you, that I have set before you life and death, blessing and cursing: therefore choose life that both you and your seed may live.—* Deuteronomy 30:19 KJV

Imagination and Imagery

From the beginning of time nothing has ever taken on material shape without first being imagined in the mind. The imagination "is of all qualities in man the most Godlike—that which associates him most closely with God" (Clark 1924). In Genesis we find the first mention of man; he is spoken of as an image. "Let us make man in our image, after our likeness." Gen.1:26 KJV. The only place where an image can be conceived is in the imagination. Man, being the highest creation of God, was a creation of God's imagination. "The source and center of all man's creative power—the power that above all others lifts him above the level of brute creation, and that gives him dominion, is his power of making images, or the power of the imagination" (Clark 1924).

Did you know that words spoken through pure imagination are creative and able to heal on many levels? Imagination is the act or power of forming mental images of what is not actually present. Guided imagery is based on the concept that your body and mind are connected. Using all of your senses, your body seems to respond as though what you are imagining is real. An example often used is to imagine an orange or a lemon in great detail—the smell, the color, and the texture of the peel. Continue to imagine the smell of the orange, and then see yourself taking a bite of the orange. Feel the cool juice from the orange activating all your taste buds. This exercise demonstrates how your body can respond to what you are imagining. It can promote relaxation, relieve stress, lower blood pressure, relieve symptoms, stimulate the immune system, reduce pain and anxiety, and promote healing. This relaxed state may allow for more control over emotions and thought processes, which may improve attitude, health, and a sense of well-being.

Imagination is your innate creative power to create something out of nothing. A message can be sent from the higher centers of the brain—where images are located—to the lower centers, which regulate physiologic functions such as breathing, heart rate, blood pressure, digestion, and temperature. Albert Einstein believed that his imagination was more important than knowledge. He knew it was the key to spiritual transformation. When the imagination becomes pure or transparent, it can reflect the goodness of spirit. Helping patients use their imaginations can be a therapeutic tool in the healing process and can help them become sensitive to what is going on in their bodies. Suggesting positive images allows the patient to send healing vibrations from the imagination through the body to promote the healing process.

I like to use a simple metaphor of a rainbow in a blue sky and allow patients to choose the color that feels the most soothing, relaxing, and healing. Then I ask them to imagine the color flowing from the rainbow into the body as a warm, liquid light. I guide them to imagine the warm, liquid light slowly flowing from the top of the head through the body—to every muscle, cell, and fiber of their being. By using their imaginations to create positive images, patients have had success in reducing pain, anxiety, and fear. Imagery is a valuable tool that offers the patient a bridge to heal the body, soul, and spirit. A recent study published in the Engineering and Technology Magazine November, 2013 discovers that paralyzed stroke patients can practice mental imagery to help reactivate damaged regions of the brains controlling use of their arms and hands.

The first step is to go beyond the natural mind or way of thinking into the creative mind or imagination. The next step is to clear the mind of all the negative thoughts and misconceptions that the natural mind may be preoccupied with. We are continuously receiving pictures and images from our environment and our subconscious mind. It is important to keep the canvas of our imagination clean for the artwork of the spirit to be painted on it. When the imagination is activated by spirit, it unleashes creativity, heightened perception, new ideas, and possibly even inventions. The possibilities are endless. An active faith will determine how you interact and what you imagine in the quantum field of potential and possibilities. The unseen realm, from which all is created, determines what manifests to become your reality. A vision is looking into the future and seeing it as God sees it. It is the invisible substance from which your physical world of reality is being created. Getting this information is like data reaching you from your future potential faster than the speed of light.

All things are possible to him that believes.—Mark 9:23 KJV

Sacred Creative Words

He sent his word and healed them.

—Psalm 107:20 KJV

The scriptures tell us that our words are important and should be considered before we speak them. The prophet Malachi tells us that God keeps a book of remembrance of our words. The seer and dream interpreter, Daniel, was told by the angel Gabriel that he had come for his words to carry them out, or make them a reality. Angels are listening to our words waiting to accomplish them, or bring them to fruition.

In the opening lines of Genesis, we see the Creator performing an awesome work of creation by first speaking the word into existence. He said, "Let us make man in our image, according to our likeness; let them have dominion or authority." Genesis says he breathed the breath of life into the creature, and he became a living being. In the Hebrew translation, it means "a speaking spirit." We are not just physical creatures; we also have a spiritual component able to speak words creatively. Evil forces do the same, but they are not creative in themselves; *we* are creative. Sometimes we give evil forces the creative material they need when we speak negative, angry words. The spirit body shines light; it gives off emissions of God's authority and radiates his energy. Although the world places great value on the intellectual mind, it is becoming more essential that we learn to function in the realm of the spirit mind, apart from human thought processes. Despite all its wisdom and abilities, mankind has utterly failed to govern itself in a way that produces righteousness and peace. "Imagination is more important than knowledge. For knowledge is limited, whereas imagination encircles the entire world, and all there ever will be to know and understand"(www.goodreads.com/quotes/tag/ablert-einstein)

STREAMS OF LIVING WATER

CHAPTER 4

PASSION AND POSSIBILITY

*If I were to wish for anything, I should not wish for wealth
and power, but for the passionate sense of what can be, for the
eye, which, ever young and ardent, sees the possible. Pleasure
disappoints possibility never. And what wine is so sparkling,
what so fragrant, what so intoxicating as possibility?*

—Soren Kierkegaard

Passion is an unusual spark of creative energy that connects
us to the unseen realm of possibilities. All around us is its
vibrancy and energy; it is continuously swirling around us.
The universe is sparking with generative power, and we are invited to
tap into the source, the Creator, and to connect with his abundant
vitality. Although it is a current of another wellspring of spirit beyond
ourselves, it is, paradoxically, within us—at our very fingertips, if we
will connect with it. Passion awakens us to an exhilarating energy
for living an abundant life. It is a life where possibilities are endless.
This awesome energy flows everywhere; it is the substance of our
spiritual existence. It's serendipitous—the phenomenon of finding
a valuable or desirable discovery that you weren't looking for. By
keeping our days simple and spontaneous, we leave ourselves open
to serendipitous adventures of spirit.

Sometimes this kind of energy may take us by surprise when we find ourselves committing to doing something extraordinary. I know a man who shared a true story of an event that happened to him several years ago. While driving in his car, he heard a call go out on the radio for an unusually rare blood type that was needed at a nearby hospital. Suddenly, he turned his car around and headed for that hospital. He knew he had the rare blood type they were asking for, and he felt a strong passion to respond to the call. The story had a happy ending. Amazingly, a five-year-old boy's life was saved that day because my friend acted on his passion. Nurses have this kind of passion; surely, it was passion that led us to care for the sick. We can participate with passion every day by learning how to give way to something much bigger than ourselves. It takes an act of surrender, a letting go, allowing ourselves to be an open vessel to shape the stream of passion into new expressions.

Here is a beautiful example from someone who had a breathtaking experience with nature's passion while on vacation:

> The river roared like mad, its waters rolling by with incessant speed and energy. The abundance was outrageous, confrontational. I could barely hear myself think. I wavered; it was impossible to be there and resist for long. To preserve myself from this nerve-racking force, ringing so loudly in my ears, I could have turned away and climbed back up to the thoroughfare; I could have found a comfortable distance. Yet, standing stationary on the bank, utterly still, I took an existential leap. "Let its force run through me," I said, not having moved an inch. "Let it turn all my molecules in its direction. Let it give me what it has to offer." And it did. Whenever I seek life's passion, the river is there, churning through me. I can hear the billions of atoms moving all at once. I asked myself, *what was nature asking me for?* Not knowing how to cope with so much beauty, so much power, I asked myself a question and—surprisingly—it brought the answer. Nature was

asking me to flow with it; it was calling me to feel the skimming of the water. It was asking me to participate.

Later that day, when she began to paint, she found that it was the momentum of nature that showed up on the canvas. It wasn't the object, the lines, or the color but the dynamic forces, geometric vibrancy, and the passion of color.

While pondering the unusual experience, she realized that she was being pulled out of her usual way of experiencing life and was asked to participate in another way, a way that was not comfortable. She was being asked to flow with spirit, which allowed her to discover a part of herself beyond the physical form. Because we are spirit, we are related to the waves in the sea and the wind that blows—and we should never lose continuity with the movement of the spirit all around us. It can be exciting to connect with it. Life flows when we put our attention on the larger patterns of which we are a part. Life takes on new shape and meaning when we are able to transcend the barriers of limitation and become a unique conduit for spirit's vital energy. The supply is all around us; as we make this shift, we become open to spontaneously flow with the momentous passion of spirit (Zander 2002).

> *I dwell in Possibility—*
> *A fairer House than Prose—*
> *More numerous of Windows-*
> *Superior for Doors-*
>
> *Of Chambers as the Cedars—*
> *Impregnable of eye—*
> *And for an everlasting Roof*
> *The Gambrels of the Sky*
>
> *Of Visitors— the fairest—*
> *For Occupation— This—*
> *The spreading wide my narrow Hands*
> *To gather Paradise—*
>
> —Emily Dickinson

Nature's Passion

Have you ever noticed that when you are traveling in the countryside, walking in the autumn woods, or near the summer ocean—you can perceive the presence of spiritual energy, the presence of the divine? It may come as an overwhelming peace or an unexplainable joy. It may even lift the stress of a burden. Nature emits sound waves of spiritual energy that are inaudible to our natural ear, yet our spirit receives them and we are changed. We can connect more easily with the spiritual realm through nature's beautiful surroundings; nature's beauty nurtures our souls. Nature brings us an unexplainable enjoyment. All of creation is here to serve us; it not only hears and understands but replies and offers us assistance. Even objects such as rocks, mountains, and trees have sound emanating from them and communicate with us through the spiritual energy around us. Scientists tell us that nothing created can be uncreated—things created only change form. According to the law of thermodynamics, for example, burned wood turns to ash but does not disappear. Although the ash seems to dissolve, it is reduced to smaller molecules that still contain embedded sound particles.

"This element (beauty) I call an ultimate end. No reason can be asked or given why the soul seeks beauty. Beauty, in its largest and profoundest self, is one expression of the universe" (Emerson 1982).

Using Passion in Creative Group Therapy and Its Effects on Depression

While working with a group of depressed patients in a creative group setting, I asked them if they could paint their passion. They were all asked to use their imagination and creativity. The theme was "If you could paint a picture of your life, what would it look like?" The outcomes were truly amazing. When they finished, several volunteers wanted to share their pictures and stories. One lady painted a cemetery and confided, "That's me in the grave." She said her intense emotional pain made her feel as if she had died, and by painting her inner reality, she gave meaning and expression to it—resulting in relief from the emotional pain.

Another lady painted a picture of herself sewing a beautiful wedding gown. She included her husband at her side and said, "It's our wedding day." She shared how happy her life was with him and how much she enjoyed her career as a dress designer and seamstress. We discovered that by painting certain memories of her life, she was able to connect to the feelings of joy and contentment that were stored in the cells of her memory bank. All of the patients who participated in the creative art group had a decrease in their level of depression and anxiety; some said it was gone completely. The creative group therapy sessions were always transforming for the patients. The results were incredible. As the patients connected with their passions through imagination and memory, then brought them onto the canvas, they experienced a release from mental anguish, fear, depression, and anxiety. This is the power of imagination to heal and transform.

What is the explanation of genius? It is the result of a soul that unconsciously goes out to God's great realm (spirit) and discovers what is already there. John G. Lake gives an account of this: while he was preaching, a minister and friend of his was listening and said that something came down and stood there. The minister said it was so visible and clear that he made a drawing of it. It was a baby bed, different from anything produced before. He went and got a patent for it. What was the secret? Simply under the inspiration of the spirit realm, his spirit entered the creative realm and produced that new baby bed (Liardon 1999).

> *There is a vitality, a life force, an energy, a quickening that is translated through you into action, and because there is only one of you in all of time, this expression is unique. And if you block it, it will never exist through any other medium*

and it will be lost. The world will not have it. It is not your business to determine how good it is nor how valuable nor how it compares with other expressions. It is your business to keep it yours clearly and directly, to keep the channel open.— Martha Graham (De Mille 1991)

CHAPTER 5

QUANTUM CONCEPTS AND PHENOMENA

"Once you can accept the universe as matter expanding into nothing that is something, wearing stripes with plaid comes easy" Albert Einstein (www.goodreads.com/author/quotes/9818,Albert)

Einstein's theory of relativity connects to the words we speak and how they affect the environment and us. Albert Einstein (1879–1955) was a German born Jewish theoretical physicist. He is best known for his theory of relativity and specifically mass energy equivalence, E is energy, and M is mass or any substance that has mass and occupies space, $E=MC^2$: Einstein was especially fascinated by the account of creation.

Quantum physics is the study of matter and energy on a subatomic level. Einstein concluded that energy is real, even though it is invisible to the naked eye. Even though we can't see electricity we know it is real when we turn on a light. Spiritual energy can also be experienced or realized—during meditation or prayer. Meditation enables us to become spiritually energized and revitalizes us physically. We create a charged atmosphere or changed vibration through meditation or prayer; this releases the potential for a "lifting up" from our natural capacity to a spiritual empowerment. Even though we may have experienced exhaustion only moments earlier, we now feel enlarged in spirit, revitalized in body, and renewed by an optimistic attitude and clear focus of mind.

Scientists who study string theory believe that the smallest particle is not the electron, the neutron, or the proton; they believe it is sound—sound waves or vibrating strings that have "notes." When you take the smallest atom known (a neutron or a proton) and split it to its smallest form, there is one more particle inside the smallest particle—a vibrating sound wave. Scientists now say that the smallest particle is a sound wave, the building block and first ingredient of all things created—including us.

Building blocks: energy fields, open system pattern, and pan dimensionality.

> Assumptions: man is a unified whole, more than the sum of his parts. Energy fields are in an open system, not causal. Energy field are pan dimensionality without spatial or temporal attribute. (Martha Rogers 1989)

An interesting account of the use of these creative powers is in the life of John G. Lake, a missionary to South Africa. The early 1900s has documented this account: many people were dying during the bubonic plague outbreak. Lake was asked why he had not contracted the disease since he used no protection of gloves or mask in the same environment as sick people. He said, "It is the spiritual energy that was being created through me that has an indestructible power of life, greater than the disease." To demonstrate, he had live bubonic plague germs—still foaming from the lungs of a newly dead person—removed and placed in his hands, and when the germs were examined under a microscope, they were dead (Liardon 1999).

There Is a Nonphysical Reality

When we consider creation and all things eternal, we find that our concepts regarding time and matter limit our understanding. Everything we see is part of a vast ocean of infinitesimally small subatomic particles. Under certain conditions, these subatomic structures also take on the properties of invisible waves. These waves or particles that make up all matter cause that matter to blink into existence by being observed by the experimenter. How can it be that these invisible elements, which make up all matter, can be changed from particles to waves by being observed? This is beyond our human consciousness and our five senses. Quantum physics indicates that there is some profound relationship between observation and the physical world.

In the 1970s, David Van Koevering, scientist and inventor, worked with Dr. Bob Moog, and together they gave the music world the first performance keyboards called Moog synthesizers. He learned to work with electrons and photons, tiny elements that are so small they can't even be seen; yet these invisible elements are how all electronic devices work. Van Koevering and Moog created the first modulated memory retrieval system. This recorded encoded information—audio and later video—and was the first step toward CDs and DVDs. This came on the market in 1983. How is it that our cameras and computers have memory, that they can remember information? Can we grasp the concept that other matter remembers information? Van Koevering says, "Our false concepts regarding time, space, and matter limit our understanding of the spiritual realm" (Von Koevering 2007). He believes quantum physics opens the door to other nonclassical physics and to the unseen world—suggesting that a large part of our universe is nonphysical. The universe is greater than science has discovered or can explain. Is this invisible world a part of the spiritual realm?

The scriptures speak of the Creator being outside of our time and calendar, looking in. He is observing and sustaining all things in this nanosecond (one billionth of a second) and is singing the frequencies or vibrations of our bodies—and if he didn't, we would dissolve. We think we are solid objects, but quantum mechanics has confirmed that all subatomic particles—the stuff we are made of—are blinking in and out of this reality. When God spoke and all the frequencies of his glory became manifest, the cosmos came into existence. From the tiniest vibrating superstring that is causing or "singing" the atoms that make up the table of 103 elements—all the way through everything the Hubble telescope sees—are the vibrating frequencies of the Creator's voice. He is before all things, meaning he is outside of time. He is the Alpha (beginning) and Omega (ending), outside our concept of time in his eternal now and causing all things to be.

A Japanese researcher and doctor of alternative medicine, Masaru Emoto, experimented with water particles and other subatomic particles. He discovered that crystals formed in frozen water reveal changes when specific, concentrated thoughts and/or words are directed toward them. Our bodies are comprised of 70–80 percent water. Emoto's findings showed that the thoughts, feelings, words, music, and even the emotions transmitted to the water particles radically affected the crystals. The crystals responded to sound and voice recognition. The music formed crystals into either a very beautiful pattern with perfect symmetry or a very horrible, chaotic pattern—depending on whether the words spoken were positive or negative. A Mozart symphony and words of love and gratitude made the crystal into a beautiful snowflake shape. Heavy metal and hard rock with words like "you make me sick" formed the crystal into a blob shape that looked almost like vomit. Emoto believed that every created thing hears, in a sense records, and then *responds* in some way. Everything ever created shares the same core ingredient—sound. Remember to speak a blessing over your food before you eat; the atoms in the food will change (Emoto 2004).

Quantum physics confirms that if you study an object long enough, it will respond in a certain way because you were observing it; the object realizes it is being observed and will change, either positively or negatively. Quantum mechanics indicates that there is an order to the universe. It simply isn't the *expected* order. Even describing the true order of the universe is difficult, because it involves something more than the physical world. It involves *us*—our minds and our thoughts. The gradual recognition that what we think may physically influence what we observe has led to a revolution in thought and philosophy, not to mention physics.

Today it is not difficult to believe that matter has memory, because most of us have tiny memory sticks or memory cards that record or store information from our cameras and computers. The phenomenon of information flowing into matter and recalling it is commonplace. Photons from all light sources reflect from our body and off our belongings. And these information-carrying photons go into *all* matter, including walls, your watch, or a ring. This information—even what we say and think—is modulating or moving through the connectedness of all atomic structures. Every word, action, and deed done in the flesh has been recorded. This is where yesterday went. All events past are recorded and stored in matter and will someday be played back.

Mathematical Equations = Musical Notes

In essence, String Theory describes space and time. Matter and energy, gravity and light, indeed all of God's creation . . . as music.

—Roy H. Williams

NASA scientists recently discovered that sound waves of musically harmonious notes were coming from black holes, which are collapsed stars. Other experiments have revealed similar results from rock samples taken from outer space. In fact, they discovered that every created thing has musical sound waves embedded in it. Sound waves today have magnificent uses in our modern day lives, especially in medicine where they are used to destroy cancer cells. During the black hole study, scientists detected sounds emanating from a black hole. Why would musical sounds be produced from creation? Even rock samples from distant planets emit sounds we can hear when we put them under special machines that track sound waves and energy. Scientists say that our DNA is based on mathematical equations that express who we are and that these mathematical equations can be decoded into musical notes. Is it possible we are a unique song vibrating in the universe? As tiny as we may seem, the Creator—who knows every star by name—also knows your name and mine.

Did angels initiate the songs, or did they merely begin to sing in harmony with the master quantum physicist as he sang creation into existence? The allegory *The Magician's Nephew*, by C. S. Lewis, is a fictional account of the creation and is perhaps much closer to the truth than we might first think. Lewis suggests that God *sang* his creative commands over the void, rather than just speaking the words. Lewis recalls—as written in the scriptures—that during creation angels were singing and rejoicing at the marvelously skillful handiwork of the Creator. God asked Job, "Where were you when I laid the earth's foundation? Tell me, if you understand. Who marked off its dimensions? Surely you know! Who stretched a measuring line across it? On what were its footings set, or who laid its cornerstone—*while the morning stars sang together and all the angels shouted for joy?*" (Job 38:4–7 NIV).

It is quite compelling to consider that the voice of God that resounds over the entire universe could actually sustain the material world at a quantum level—by energizing and vibrating the tiny strings that some theoretical physicists believe constitute the underlying fabric of the physical order.

Several years ago, I had an experience that inspired my curiosity about sound waves and nonphysical reality. I discovered that sound can be a bridge between the two realms of time and eternity. While hearing a choir perform Handel's Messiah, a soloist's voice broke that sound barrier between heaven and earth, and at once the walls in the room were gone. There were a myriad of angels standing where the walls had just been, and when I looked up, the ceiling was gone and I was seeing into eternity. I saw a circle up in the universe, and I knew God dwelled there. That day, I discovered for myself that there is a nonphysical reality and that we have the capacity to be in more than one place or realm at a time.

An Observer-Created Reality

> *If quantum mechanics hasn't profoundly shocked you, you haven't understood it yet.*
>
> —Niels Bohr

Fred Alan Wolf—physicist, author, and lecturer—is well known for his simplification of quantum physics. He describes how our consciousness transforms quantum wave functions into the particles and atoms that make up physical reality as we know it. He calls it "poppin' the quiff"—*quiff* being short for "quantum wave function."

Wolf says, "Although there is controversy among quantum physicists in extrapolating what we see on the quantum level to life on a bigger level, it fits in with what we deliberate creators have learned about manifesting our reality."

Instead of pinpointing the building blocks of life as microcosmic "things" that are easy to understand and predict, scientists found "waves of possibilities," also described as "vibrating energy packets." It seems these quantum waves remained in that state until someone took a measurement of them—until an observer showed up. That act of observation or the influence of consciousness (as some argue), is what transforms possibility into reality. Wolf says, "All the possibilities are there, as quantum wave functions. So we have before us all possibilities, and we draw forth a particular possibility by focusing on it. That 'pops the quiff'—the quantum wave function—into the prickly particles we know as 'reality.' If we truly understand that anything is possible, and that all we have to do is choose it in order to experience it, I have a feeling we'd get a little more open— maybe even daring and creative—about what we choose." Wolf says, "Pretty cool way of thinking about it, huh?" (goodvibeblog.com./ what-quiff-are-you-poppin/).

This understanding has brought about a shift from a belief in the independent existence of the material universe to a belief in the subjective observer who, by consciously observing the universe, gives reality to the material world. In this process, there has been a shift from the supremacy of materialism to the supremacy of consciousness over matter. Quantum physics now shows us that we are not insignificant creatures subject to the random forces of an immense universe after all. In fact, it says just the opposite. It says that the behavior of the basic component of all natural reality (atoms) depends on us (Hicks 2012).

The following is an inspiring experience that supports these findings. I met John Paul Jackson—a theologian, prophet, and lecturer from Texas—at a conference I attended in Franklin, Tennessee last summer. He gave an account of being taken to heaven and standing about eight feet from the throne of God. He said, "When you're there you just know things, and I just knew I was eight feet from the throne." He described it this way:

The atmosphere was filled with divine creative energy and charged with the presence of the glory of the Creator. The possibilities were endless—miracles were the norm. I could envision mathematical equations that were brought before me—then I could easily speak the mathematical equations. When I spoke the mathematical equations into the charged atmosphere it started to form and create buildings from the words that I spoke. And although it was too much to grasp, it thrilled me.

As this new century unfolds, we are finally coming to grips with what Werner Heisenberg first noticed back in the 1920s: "Atoms are not things, they are tendencies" (Scientific American, January 2005). The concentrated research of the past eighty years has confirmed that the basic components of the physical reality we inhabit (atoms) require instructions before they will form the electromagnetic fields that comprise our physical universe. This statement is universal. It refers to all atoms. Not only does everything made by human beings require a conscious observer to first imagine and then make "real" what "are only tendencies" but the existence of every atom in the universe also adheres to the same requirement. This includes the atoms that make up you, me, and the galaxies on the other side of the universe (Hicks 2012). "God . . . calls into existence the things that do not exist" (Roman 4:17 ESV).

The law that calls into being in this outer material world everything that is real in the inner world is the 'conception' of what can be. What we believe is the material of which our future is made. Hebrews 11:1 states, "Now faith (what you believe) is the substance of things hoped for, the evidence of things not seen" (KJV). All things are possible if a person believes that what they imagine will, in fact, become a real occurrence in this physical reality.

Irene Fulmer, RN

A person's body is confined in time and space, but the mind and soul are not confined to the physical universe. One's higher sense of mind and soul transcends time and space and helps to account for notions like collective unconsciousness, casual past, mystical experiences, parapsychological phenomena, miracles, and a higher sense of power and may be an indicator by numerous philosophers, including Teilhard de Chardin, Kierkegaard, Hegel, and Marce (DeChardin 1967). Indicating that humans are evolving toward an "omega point" to become more holy, more God-conscious. (Jean Watson 2012)

CHAPTER 6

ORDINARY ACTS OF KINDNESS

Each person has inside a basic decency and goodness. If he listens to it and acts on it, he is giving a great deal of what it is the world needs most. It is not complicated but it takes courage. It takes courage for a person to listen to his own goodness and act on it.

—Pablo Casals

The uncovering of this "law of kindness" was the catalyst for this book. It stirred within me, yet I knew of no such law. Kindness is the discovering of the explosive power we all have at our fingertips . . . a simple act of kindness. It seems so simple, maybe even ordinary; yet kindness emerges as one of the most powerful tools we have within our everyday lives. It can literally change the world if we choose to use it. With kindness, we can go beyond the ordinary to the extraordinary.

Emanuel Swedenborg, a Swedish scientist and philosopher, said that "kindness" was an inner desire that makes us want to do good things, even if we don't get anything in return. He said it brings joy to our lives to do them and creates a peaceful, positive environment. When we show kindness, it multiplies—and enacts the potential for more growth. Our society has become preoccupied with materialism and secularism. We have emphasized knowledge and education, and yet it seems we still haven't learned the simple yet profound importance of practicing kindness. Ralph Waldo Emerson measured his success by how often he showed kindness and shared with others, even strangers. Kindness is a virtue and has healing power; it touches us on what is probably the deepest level of our existence: the soul and spirit. It mends, soothes, heals, and changes those to whom we offer it. Kindness creates a flow of compassion; it opens the deeper mystery that we are all connected and that what we experience is shared. On this foundational level, we have possibility to heal each other. The famous Muppet character, Kermit the frog, called it the "rainbow connection;" he said that wherever he goes and whomever he meets, he considers them his family.

Kindness works! It changes you, the recipient, and the atmosphere so that even those in the vicinity are affected by the positive energy vibrations it emits. Stagnant water that is losing life doesn't benefit anyone, but a flowing river will give way to an abundant life. The heart and the will control kindness. Letting the water flow to access it is a decision we make. We can choose to be open and extend a helping hand, or we can remain closed like stagnant water and miss the opportunity. Our fears can cause us to rationalize and say, "I don't even know you—you are a stranger," causing us to remain in our familiar zone.

Remember what happened after 9/11? There was a mass merge of togetherness, and everyone seemed to care more about one another. Drivers on the road were more courteous; people were more open and approachable. It was happening everywhere, in stores and shopping centers, on trains, subways, and on the streets. We were no longer strangers. We were more comfortable with each other. It didn't seem to matter what color, age, religion, or nationality you were; the dividing walls were down, and we understood—we are all in this together. An awareness and acknowledgment of God increased that day. God became part of our daily conversation. Prayers were spoken, inspired songs were sung, and candles were lit in honor of the missing and perished souls. We shared a corporate burden in our hearts, we cried together, and we comforted one another. Churches that were usually empty experienced an overflow of visitors, especially in the lower Manhattan area. How do we explain this phenomenon? Shall we say, for a brief moment, that we left our delusions of separateness? Maybe.

The legendary Mother Teresa's work helping the poor has become the measuring rod by which the entire world measures kindness, compassion, selflessness, and generosity of heart. In 1950, she founded the Order of Missionaries of Charity, a Roman Catholic group of women dedicated to helping the poor. In 1979, she won the Nobel Peace Prize and in 1985 was awarded the Medal of Freedom—the highest civilian award in the United States. Mother Teresa's words and acts of kindness have inspired millions of people all over the world to help the poor and needy, the sick and dying, transcending the barriers of race, religion, and ethnicity.

> *Live as if everything you do will eventually become known.*— Hugh Prather

Mother Teresa once said that the reason she was given the Nobel Prize was because of the poor. She said the prize went beyond appearances. In fact, it awakened consciences in favor of helping the poor all over the world. It became a reminder that the poor are our brothers and sisters and those we have the duty to treat with love.

> *I was sick and you took care of Me.*—Matthew 25:35–36 KJV Cambridge edition

Mother Teresa said that when we care for the sick and dying, we are taking care of God.

It can be as simple as listening to someone in need and responding. Nurses do this every day. I once watched a nurse weep with a mother whose twenty-seven-year-old son was dying. The mother said, "You have comforted me with your tears of compassion—I will never forget your kindness." I observed Mary, an ICU nurse, hold a patient's hand while she was taking her last breath. She took the bedside picture of her family and placed it in the patient's hand to hold; then she prayed the "Our Father" prayer into her ear. I once witnessed a surgeon weep with a husband after he lost his wife in childbirth.

> *Not all of us can do great things. But we can do small things with great love.*—Mother Teresa

The Smile: A Universal Language

We should smile more often. Does it take us out of our comfort zone to smile? Or is it our hurried lives that don't allow us time to smile? Sometimes it is hard for us to smile because we are tired, stressed, or feel vulnerable to reach out to others or strangers. A smile not only brings comfort and joy, but also it conveys a sense of belonging for both the giver and the receiver. Did you know that eyes can smile? People with joy in their hearts have smiling eyes. Let's not forget the enormous potential of a smile: "Strength and dignity are her clothing, and she smiles at the future. She opens her mouth in wisdom, and the teaching of kindness is on her tongue" (Proverbs 31:25–26 amplified version).

What are the health benefits of training yourself to smile? Researchers are finding that wearing a smile brings certain health benefits, like slowing down the heart rate and reducing stress. This may even happen when people aren't aware they are forming a smile, according to a recent study. The study was published in the *Psychological Science* November 2012 and found that people who smiled after they engaged in stress-inducing tasks showed a greater reduction in heart rate than people who maintained a neutral facial expression. "We smile because we feel not threatened," says Dr. Pressman. Over time that message evolved so the muscle activity involved in a smile sent a message to the brain, signaling safety, which we've already seen translate into lower heart rates and stress levels. Dr. Pressman is currently researching how smiling affects stress hormones, such as cortisol and oxytocin, which is sometimes called the trust hormone.

Paul Ekman, a professor emeritus of psychology at the University of California in San Francisco, believes only a genuine smile confers health benefits. He says such a smile activates major muscles around the mouth and the eyes. It generates the physiology of positive emotion and the changes in the brain associated with spontaneous enjoyment.

Marco Iacoboni, a lab director at the UCLA Brain Mapping Center, says, "People who smile have a real positive impact on others. When people smile, so-called mirror neurons fire in their brain and evoke a similar neural response as if they were smiling themselves."

Showing Kindness to Our Self

The visionary priest Pierre Teilhard de Chardin defined *human holiness* as one's soul possessing a body that is not confined by objective space and time—and that the personality, the ego, is here to carry forth the energy of the spirit or higher sense of self. He spoke of how important it was to take good care of our *self* in order to fulfill that purpose. Spending time in prayer and meditation allows us to access the true essence of our being, which is neither our ego nor our thoughts; in fact, it has nothing to do with our career or social status, either. It is the essence or substance of that which lives on into eternity. It is our spirit, and it is already perfect and whole.

Self-care is probably the most important "care" for nurses and all health-care professionals, because we take care of the sick and dying. Having the ability to love ourselves is frequently the biggest hindrance to caring for our *self.* This attitude has pervaded not just nursing; it has pervaded many cultures and societies. Whether conscious or unconscious, our attitude is that we are not quite deserving of being loved. As nurses, our role is in giving, making sacrifices, and many times we feel guilty about taking care of *ourselves*. Nurses need to embrace their profession as sacred and to embrace the reality that they are valuable human beings with spirits made in the image and likeness of the Creator. This makes our physical bodies quite valuable, since they are the vehicles whereby our spirits can come through us.

In *Nursing: Human Science and Human Care*, Jean Watson wrote, "My conception of life and personhood is tied to notions that one's soul possesses a body that is not confined by objective space and time . . . there is a great deal of regard, respect, and awe given to the concept of a human soul (spirit or higher sense of self) that is greater than the physical, mental, and emotional existence of a person at any given point in time." The personality or ego is here to carry out the purpose of the spirit or higher self. Therefore, we must take good care of ourselves in order to fulfill that higher purpose. Spending time in prayer, contemplation, and meditation allows us to access the essence of who we are and to discover our true destiny. We are already perfect; our spirit is immortal, and it sustains and quickens our mortal bodies.

Taking Kindness to a Third-World Nation

> *Do not neglect to show hospitality to strangers, for you may be entertaining angels unaware.*
> —Hebrews 13:2 ESV

Several years ago, my friends Betty and Richard invited me to go to Zambia, Africa to do some good will work for Zambia's "poorest of the poor" in the McKinsey Compound.

The compound is home to approximately five thousand people, more than two hundred of whom are orphaned children. Visiting Zambia was a wonderful experience for me, one that I will not forget anytime soon. Although Zambians have virtually no material possessions, they are very rich in spiritual essence. Zambian faces light up with beautiful smiles—whether they are children or adults—and their eyes are filled with faith and hope revealing the fire of God within their hearts. They have surely won a place in my heart.

When I arrived, I was welcomed at the home of Peter and Rodie, a very gracious husband and wife, originally from Sir Lanka and now living in Zambia. Although Peter is a banker, they provide guesthouses to missionaries from all over the world. My first sense of life in Zambia was the mournful sound of a woman weeping. There is sacredness in tears. They are messengers of overwhelming grief and love. The universal language of pain gripped my heart too. She was the housekeeper at Rodie and Peter's home and had just heard the news of her twenty-seven-year-old son's death to the AIDS virus. An estimated eight hundred seventy thousand are infected with HIV, and the estimated total number of children orphaned by AIDS is six hundred fifty thousand. More than 80 percent of those living with HIV/AIDS are aged twenty to twenty-nine years. Life expectancy has dropped from sixty to forty-two years.

The McKinsey Compound Clinic consisted of a very small room with cement walls and floors, a bench for the sick to sit on while waiting for treatment, a sheet hanging for privacy, and a small table to dispense medication. About sixty adults and children visited the compound each day. Cases of cholera, worms, scabies, AIDS, tuberculosis, and malaria were noted. They brought used washed-out bottles and jars to carry the medicine home. Working with Violet—an RN who donated her time to the clinic—was a wonderful experience for me. She translated the Bemba language for me, so I was able to understand their stories. We diagnosed, wrote medication orders, and dispensed the medicine. There, people bow to you with gratitude. They were grateful for the many donations of medicine and medical supplies from the North Shore Hospital at Syosset/Plainview, New York where I work.

I had an opportunity to visit the Ndola Central Hospital in Zambia. It held nine hundred beds, of which only six hundred fifty were in use. Since the government subsidizes them, the wages were low, and only two doctors worked there. A nurse made thirty dollars a month; a doctor made fifty. There were no specialists. The health-care conditions were at least seventy years—if not a century—behind America. Most of the surgeries were done in South Africa. I met a woman who had to go to South Africa to see an ophthalmologist because there were none in Zambia. I had the opportunity to meet with the hospital's executive director, Dr. Jabbin L. Mulwanda. He was grateful for our donations of medicine and supplies. He said, "You have so much, and we have so little."

One evening, Peter and Rodie took us to Peter's boss's home for dinner. Dr. Matauni is one of the richest men in Zambia. His gracious hospitality afforded us a lovely evening. While we were saying our goodbyes, Dr. Matauni asked if I could pray for his feet. He was in great pain from a gout condition. The moment I placed my hands on his feet, I could feel the power of spiritual virtue flow into his feet. The next morning, I met his lawyer at the airport; she was also flying to Lusaka. She mentioned that Dr. Matauni had been speaking with great gratitude, as the pain in his feet was completely gone after the prayer. In his generosity and gratitude, he upgraded my ticket back to the States to first class. It humbled me as I recognized that to be a demonstration of God's favor on my life.

I saw several other healings and miracles during my visit to Zambia. One day, we visited an orphanage in Zambia where seven children lived. Grace and Ruby were the children's caregivers. They were all so happy to see us, as they didn't have many visitors coming from the States. Ruby's home was in Canada; when she saw us, she was reminded of how much she missed her family. She hugged us and cried; it was a very emotional experience for all of us. Ruby was homesick; she hadn't been back to her family in over three years. During our visit, Grace confided in me about her heart condition. She said there was fluid around her heart and asked if we could pray. As soon as I took her hands, we were both struck by the power of God flowing through our bodies. We literally dropped to the floor. Grace's health began to improve considerably in the days that followed.

At one of the worship meetings, a lady came to me and asked me to pray for the pain all over her body. We prayed and I again felt the power of God's virtue go to her. The next day she came to me saying all her pain was gone. I think I was more amazed than she was. I remember thinking; *can I bring this special healing anointing back to America?*

Peter and Rodie's eleven-year-old son Richard had malaria. He was sick in bed with a fever and pain from an exacerbation of the disease. When I prayed for him, we both felt the powerful, healing virtue flowing to him. The next day, when I inquired about Richard, Rodie said his fever had broken, the pain was gone, and he had gone to school.

You shall lay your hands on the sick and they shall recover.— Mark 16:18 KJV

Robert Bartow copyright 2006

DAYBREAK

CHAPTER 7

IS IT THE DAWNING
OF A NEW AGE?

For as the Heavens are higher than the earth, so are my ways
higher than your ways, and my thoughts than your thoughts.
—Isaiah 55:8–9

O ver time we have come to understand that life is a process
of ever-unfolding cycles of change. Nature so beautifully
portrays this in the changing of seasons. As these cycles
of change have redressed our landscape over time, there remains
a theme, an invisible thread that appears again and again. Since
we are on the inside of time's dimension, we have a limited view
of its spiritual significance. The spiritual realm is all around us
yet our perception is limited; we have difficulty understanding
spiritual phenomena and how the divine interacts in our daily lives.
There is a biblical account of the prophet Ezekiel's vision of a wheel
within a wheel. Ezekiel's vision gives us some understanding of the
simultaneous interaction of the two realms of earth and heaven. The
prophet describes a big wheel—the will of God—acting upon the
smaller wheel, which is our life on earth. We discover that we have
a destiny to fulfill. As we come into alignment with this heavenly
purpose, it brings us to several conclusions: 1) we are not alone,
2) there is always help for us, and 3) there is a heavenly mandate

entwined within our everyday events. This new awareness increases our capacity to interact with the divine and offers new meaning and excitement to our existence.

Our spirit bodies exist outside of time and space and are much larger than our natural bodies. Our natural bodies have five senses that connect us to this world; our spiritual bodies also have five or more senses, connecting us to the *spiritual* world—and the veil between the two is getting thinner as we move into the future.

These two planes or realms of consciousness in which we live make up the natural, limited realm, where we operate out of the ego or self-consciousness. Since we are born into the natural realm, our human experience limits us to this natural state of existence, and we are unaware that there is more. In our natural experience, we have a great variety of ups and downs, some goodness and weaknesses of character. Yet there can be a practical application for overcoming or rising above each circumstance.

The other plane is the spiritual realm. It will require a great shift of consciousness—a transformation or metamorphosis—if we are to live and fully operate in this spiritual dimension. The realm of spirit is an unlimited dimension, not subject to the laws here on earth. It has the power to elevate our consciousness to a higher perspective so that we are removed from our natural mind or natural way of thinking, into our *spirit* mind or God's thoughts. Some hindrances from the natural realm of existence are: pride, envy, hatred, strife, and division. The process of discovering who we are from the higher plane of spirit frees us from the natural limitations that see only by outward appearance. It removes the spots and blemishes of our earthly or lower nature and allows us to become partakers of our higher or divine nature. Some virtues of the spirit are: patience, gentleness, forbearance, meekness, love, peace, goodness, strength, and joy.

Paradise Lost and Paradise Regained

To understand what actually happened to the earth and its inhabitants we need to go back to the book of beginnings—Genesis, where the story begins. In the beginning, man's spirit was the dominant force in this world. When God spoke the universe into existence, his entire bandwidth of glory was made physical. From his glory (all frequencies) and his voice (all frequencies expressed), all light, energy, and matter came into existence. The speed of light is believed to be 186,000 miles per second. The spiritual realm operates above the speed of light. The physical realm was shaped to its current limits by the fall. After the fall, Adam and Eve lost their bandwidth—and in their fall downward, they lost their spiritual consciousness. The speed of light slowed down, and they lost their compatibility with God by the great deceiver. When God asked Adam where he was, it wasn't because he didn't know; he wanted Adam to know he was aware of his fallen state. It resulted from the choice Adam and Eve made to touch the forbidden tree. The tasting of its fruit opened Adam's awareness and senses to a lower realm of consciousness—the knowledge of good and evil. Because they lost their compatibility with God, they were banned from the garden of paradise, and the gate was closed.

But God had a remedy, and at the end of the story in Revelation (an apocalypse or mystery revealed) we discover that the deceiver loses his power to deceive mankind. The gate to the garden opens, and paradise is regained; an environment where we can experience or know God is restored. In this restoration, mankind can receive his bandwidth back through the spirit and begin to understand God's plan for mankind.

A World in Chaos

The world is in a time of global shaking and instability. Nations rise against nations, wars, and rumors of wars. Scientists predict that since human life and human consciousness are intrinsically one with the life of the planet—as the old consciousness decreases—there will be synchronistic geographic and climatic natural upheavals in many parts of the world. In the past fifty years alone, earthquakes have exponentially increased in frequency, occurring almost daily. The big 7.0 earthquake in Haiti in 2010 had three hundred sixteen thousand fatalities. In March 2011, Japan had a catastrophic 9.0 earthquake followed by the tsunami, resulting in a total of 20,352 fatalities. The state of Virginia had a 5.8 earthquake in August 2011, sending shock waves up the entire east coast into Canada. California has had thirty-one earthquakes in the past twenty years (en.wikipedia. org/wikiListfofearthquakes). Almost daily, natural disasters strike our planet: tsunamis, tornadoes, hurricanes, plagues, and famines. The temperature of the magma of the earth is causing the water temperature to rise under the ocean. This rising temperature is causing sudden mass deaths of fish. In March, Rio de Janeiro reported eighty tons of dead fish. Birds and other animals have begun dying in record numbers for no apparent reason. Large meteors are falling, and now scientists are warning of an asteroid hitting the earth. Changes in climate, resulting in drought and massive flooding, as we have recently seen in Colorado, have wreaked havoc on whole cultures. More than half the world's population is hungry. NASA tells us to "look up" for signs in the sky over the next several years. The first sign is Comet Ison. NASA says it is the brightest comet ever, coming closest to the sun on God's Feast of Lights, Hanukkah, November 28, 2013. Unfortunately, Comet Ison disintegrated during its swing around the Sun. There are four blood moons or lunar eclipses (when the moon passes into the shadow of the earth). Two are coming on God's feast days—Passover, April 15, 2014, and Sukkot or the Feast of Tabernacles, October 8, 2014. Two more lunar eclipses are coming on God's feast day—Passover, April 4, 2015, and Sukkot, September 28, 2015. A solar eclipse which occurs when the Moon passes between the Sun and the Earth and the Moon fully or partially blocks the

Sun will appear on March 20, 2015. Scientist Gill Broussard predicts Planet X, (planetary body) will fly by earth in March 2016. Are these signs in the heavens a signal that something big is coming? "And I will show wonders in the heavens and in the earth: Blood and fire and pillars of smoke. The sun shall be turned into darkness, and the moon into blood, before the coming of the great and awesome day of the Lord" (Joel 2:30–31 NKJV). "And there will be great earthquakes in various places, and various famine and pestilences; and there will be fearful sights and great signs from heaven" (Luke 21:11 NIV).

Our American culture is a cauldron of chaos and confusion. It is plagued by a passion to possess. The good life is found in the accumulation of things. The complexity of rushing to achieve and accomplish and accumulate more threatens to overwhelm us. The fast pace of the world accentuates our sense of being strained and hurried. Possessions and money have become more important than people. Moral decay and political corruptions abound. Political correctness is silencing our voice on important issues that people need to hear about. The very fabric of our nation is being shredded.

In such a time as this, either faith or fear will control us. We must make the choice: will we embrace peace or panic? The battlefield is our mind, and we must focus our mind and heart on the peace that is greater than outer circumstances. The power of peace is greater than all our fears, and it is strong enough to keep us through the storm. Peace and tranquility are not found in a prescription pill from the local pharmacy. They are found in our turning within, to a capacity where spirit is our supply. We are not to be troubled or afraid. Inner peace calms the storm and makes us unshakable—solid as a rock.

Pope John XXIII found the valuable secret of living life in simplicity. He said, "The older I grow the more clearly I perceive the dignity and winning beauty of simplicity in thought, conduct, and speech: a desire to simplify all that is complicated and to treat everything with the greatest naturalness and clarity." Foster(2005). The demands of life can cause frustration and bring us to exhaustion;

we can lose our faith and hope. If you have difficulty trusting God then trust the nature of God; his nature is love, and it governs everything he does. The power of love can have great influence over our everyday circumstances. It constrains our natural reactions to conflicts and gives us the power to withhold negative thoughts and reactions to difficult situations and people. To choose to love means we let go of the fears and frustrations that dominate us, allowing us to enter into a place of peace and triumph. Be the love and peace bringers to this troubled world.

Be still and know that I am God.—Psalm 46:10 KJV

A Spiritual Awakening on the Horizon

Many believe we are nearing the end of an age and awakening to a new age, the kingdom age or reign of God. This is where God comes on the scene to show us what his rule over the affairs of men is like. For thousands of years, the world has been ruled by greed, selfishness, control, hate, and so on. At this time in history, there is a battle of light clashing with darkness, and they are on a collision course. There are governmental power struggles to rule over the earth and mankind. Some governments are falling, while others are rising. We have seen this unrest spread throughout the Middle East, as dictators have been overthrown only to find more severe tyrants taking their places. The battleground is ultimately Jerusalem; the world will become more and more focused on that land, God's eternal city, as the age comes to a close. By outward appearances, it looks like political wars and the dividing of land, but it is actually a great spiritual battle. Principalities and powers are fighting for control—first over the governments of the world, next over mankind and ultimately it will reach its final battle over Jerusalem, the city of God.

In 1867, Charles Dickens wrote of a similar period of time when he published, *A Tale of Two Cities*. It began with "It was the best of times, it was the worst of times, it was the age of wisdom, it was the age of foolishness, it was the epoch of belief, it was the epoch of incredulity, it was a season of Light, it was the season of Darkness, it was the spring of hope, it was the winter of despair, we had everything before us, we had nothing before us, we were all going direct to Heaven, we were all going direct the other way" (1867).

The comparison of paradoxes back then with the present day is strikingly similar.

We are well into the days of the simultaneous increase of darkness and light. Both seeds of good and evil are coming to full maturity; we will witness the noblest and the vilest. This generation will witness the glory of heaven—with miracles, signs from the heavens, and wonders on the earth. The spirit of wisdom and revelation will enable all to know God, his nature (which is love), his grandeur, and his majesty. At the present time, our knowledge of the Creator is only about 1 percent in the earth. According to the sacred writings, this will change—and the knowledge of God's glory will cover the earth as the waters cover the sea (Habakkuk 2:14 KJV). Almost everyone will have knowledge and understanding of God. A great spiritual awakening—a reformation that will change the very core of society and bring a whole new era—is already on the horizon. As one day grows dim, the other is getting brighter.

A pastor and friend, Paul Keith Davis, tells his account:

> As I entered the sanctuary, with that first step, I was seeing both the natural and spiritual realms at the same time. Although my natural eyes still viewed the people as they worshipped, my spiritual eyes were opened to look into the spirit realm, where I observed angels standing from one corner of the building across the back of the other corner. The angels appeared to be about six to seven feet tall and wore white robes reaching to their feet. They stood approximately six feet apart and had golden belts that seemed to be made of a material resembling rope,

while others had golden sashes of the exact same color that draped across their chests. Their countenances were very compassionate and caring.

Amazed at their stature and awed by the angels, he asked, "God, who are these angels, and why have they come?" He immediately got the answer, "These are angels that gather. They are sent to gather the harvest of souls as the present age comes to a close." The *sacred* writings say that the whole earth is groaning and in travail for this day to come. All of creation, including nature, is waiting to be restored.

The Coming Paradigm Shift

As this new era or shift of consciousness takes place for mankind, it will end our current belief system as we know it. This higher consciousness goes deeper than our thoughts; it transcends all thought. Our natural mind or natural way of thinking connects us to the ego or self-consciousness, but this is not who we are. Within ourselves, our spirit self, there is a dimension that is more vast than thought. It becomes activated when we learn to live from our spirit. It is the interior region or the God within us. As our soul is touched by heaven or spirit, our minds and emotions become renewed; when we are able to receive the thoughts of spirit, we become heavenly minded. Since our spirit dwells in a realm beyond time and space, we must develop an awareness of our spirit; it is in this consciousness— of dwelling in our spirit—that we can have access to the heavenly realm. It is here in our spirit that we have dominion over the mind's thoughts, the body, and the unseen evil forces that work against us. It is in our spirit that we overcome.

Age-old bible prophecies that speak of the new heaven and earth have now become relevant to our modern times. They speak of the simultaneous collapse of the existing world order, the coming of a new heaven and earth. These prophecies refer to the inner dimension of the spirit consciousness—the kingdom reign or ruling authority of spirit that is within us. Our outer manifestation in form always reflects the inner spirit. John the Revelator spoke of a new heaven and a new earth, declaring the emergence of a transformed state of human consciousness and its new reflection in the physical realm.

> And I John, saw a new heaven and a new earth, for the former earth had passed away and there no longer existed any sea. And I saw the holy city the new Jerusalem, descending out of heaven from God, all arrayed like a bride adorned for her husband. Then I heard a mighty voice from the throne saying, See the abode of God is with men, and he will live among them, they shall be his people and he shall personally be with them and be their God. God shall wipe away all tears from their eyes, and death shall be no more, neither shall there be anguish (sorrow or mourning) nor grief nor pain anymore, for the old conditions and former order of things have passed away. And he who sits on the throne says, see, I make all things new. (Revelation 21:1–4 AB)

> Government and Peace are connected, because peace comes from order and order comes from government. This is why the millennial reign will be a reign of peace, because God's order/government will be established. For example, when a region is at war with rebellion and disarray, we want to bring peace and order. This means going in and setting up some form of government that people are willing to submit to. The Kingdom of God is also a government. Unlike the governments of this current age, the Kingdom of God is a government that is pure, righteous and perfect, but it is only in effect where it is welcomed and received. That is his covenant of peace to mankind. (Jablonowski 2006)

CHAPTER 8

LEADING BY EXAMPLE DEVELOPING THE QUALITIES FOR AUTHENTIC LEADERSHIP

Scholars tell us that genuine kindness is an attribute of the world's most successful leaders. That kindness demonstrates a powerful confidence in ourselves and in those we lead. The authors of the book, *Leading with Kindness*, identify six ingredients of kindness: compassion, integrity, gratitude, authenticity, humility, and humor.

Authors William Baker and Michael O'Malley say that great leaders are *givers* and that there are four qualities that great leaders are able to instill in others: self-confidence, self-awareness, self-control, and self-determination. They say authentic leaders provide a positive example and offer a cornerstone for moral truth and reality. They are open and sensitive to the needs and concerns of others. This capacity comes from the leaders' ability to focus fully on others, without getting sidetracked by their own issues or becoming preoccupied with their own needs. Good leaders are humble and charitable; they are not self-centered. Narcissistic leaders are preoccupied with their self-importance and power. They expect others to agree and usually surround themselves with people who are willing to comply. They are not charitable people and create an environment that is cold and disconnected from reality. Sometimes leaders mistakenly think of their elevated status as personal worthiness, self-importance, or entitlement. The reality is that our positions are only part of who we are; it is our character that truly defines us. Ability may get us to the top, but it takes character to keep us there; valuing the opinions and expertise of others is the prerequisite for greatness.

Baker and O'Malley go on to say that compassion in leaders in health care is paramount. It provides nurses and other health-care workers with that extra strength and support they need to perform—whether it is overcoming personal problems, trouble at home, or job-related challenges, as in patient care. Empathy is equally important, because it demonstrates the ability to place ourselves in others' positions and to view the world through their eyes; this is much needed in leadership. Sometimes leaders get disconnected from others' cares, and they become unduly callous, even judgmental in their outlook. However, when kindness prevails in great leaders, they give us the irreplaceable gifts of confidence, control, awareness, and determination.

Kind leaders have gratitude. The Latin root of the word is *gratus*, meaning "pleasing." Two researchers in the field of gratitude, Robert Emmons, from the University of California at Davis, and Michael McCullough, from the University of Miami, explored the impact of gratitude on health and happiness, especially the correlation between gratitude and subjective well-being. They found that most people believe that gratitude enhances life by leading to "peace of mind, happiness, physical health, and deeper, more satisfying personal relationships." Gratitude and hopefulness—combined with self-confidence—have many benefits. For example, it has been shown that leaders who are optimistic versus pessimistic are better able to see multiple aspects of a situation, think flexibly, anticipate future events, proactively take action, and astutely solve problems. They concluded that to the extent that gratitude, like other positive emotions, broadens the scope of cognition and enables flexible and creative thinking, it also facilitates coping with stress and adversity. Their research showed that gratitude improves well-being in the present and allows the expanded capacity for resiliency and wisdom. Their findings also showed that gratitude could be the key practice for creating both personal and societal health (Emmons 2004).

True authentic leaders are builders; they know how to empower others and then move out of the way. They replicate themselves in others and actually encourage those under their leadership to succeed and go farther. Good leaders have nurturing qualities and understand the value of uncovering others' strengths and talents. When a nurturing environment is created, employees are happy to be there, and that kind of enthusiasm spreads. It becomes a fire of positive energy that is charged and contagious. Good leaders in nursing are passionate and positive. Nursing should be leading and lighting the way in these chaotic and exciting times of transformation and transition. More importantly, nursing is building the next generation of caregivers and leaders.

> *Example is not the main thing in influencing others. It is the only thing.*—Albert Schweitzer

CHAPTER 9

BIOGRAPHIES OF AUTHENTIC LEADERS IN NURSING AND HEALTH CARE

Our deepest fear is not that we are inadequate. Our deepest fear is that we are powerful beyond measure. It is our light, not our darkness, that most frightens us. We ask ourselves, "Who am I to be brilliant, gorgeous, talented, and fabulous? Actually, who are you not to be?" You are a child of God. Your playing small doesn't serve the world. There is nothing enlightened about shrinking so that other people won't feel insecure around you. We were born to make manifest the glory of God within us. It is not just in some of us; it is in everyone, and as we let our own light shine, we unconsciously give other people permission to do the same.
—Marianne Williamson, *A Return to Love*, 1992

The following stories involve authentic leaders and their climbs to self-actualization. Similar threads are woven through each of their lives—all having remarkable character traits that lead one to success: great generosity of spirit, deep compassion for others, humility, commitment to the cause, boldness, and vision. It is my privilege to introduce these remarkable leaders, if only on these pages.

Hattie Made Her Mark in Ghana

As a young girl, Hattie was attracted to nursing and missionary work. When she was twelve she visited a hospital and found herself inspired by the smell of alcohol; she thought, *This is so clean, I want to work with this when I grow up.* Born in 1944 in White Marsh, North Carolina, Hattie was raised by a severely harsh stepmother. She believed her difficult childhood helped her develop her strength and perseverance, enabling her to attain her many ambitions. When Hattie was nine years old, she suffered the loss of her six-year-old brother Louis to leukemia. She remembers thinking; *Medicine didn't do enough for him* and vowed that one day she would make a difference with the sick and dying. Although she was accepted into Texas University, she had to decline when her stepmother refused to let her go away to school. Instead, she attended Nassau Community on Long Island, New York and prepared herself academically with a nursing and teaching degree. Hattie had little time for any social life, as her stepmother required her to do many chores, such as cooking, cleaning, and taking care of her younger brothers and sisters. Hattie refused to become bitter about her difficult childhood and worked hard to maintain a grateful attitude.

After graduating from nursing school, Hattie vowed she would do everything in her power to help encourage young nurses to succeed in their dreams. She was hired for her first job as a nurse aide at Central General Hospital in Plainview, New York, in 1971, and she is still there forty-two years later as an assistant nursing director with its new name, North Shore Hospital at Plainview. Today Hattie sits on the advisory board at Molloy College. She is a member of the National Association of Professional Women. She also is a teacher at the Vocational Education and Extension Board.

Hattie's faith in God is strong. Her first recollection of God was when she was a young girl. She knew God was real and made room for faith and prayer to be a part of her life. By the time Hattie was well established in her career, romance came into her life. She met Reuben on a boat ride in the Great South Bay on Long Island where they were doing a church fundraiser; he later became her husband. She said that the reason they have been happily married for twenty-three years is that they respect each other.

Although she never had any children of her own, Hattie has nurtured many young girls with their struggles to become nurses. Hattie believes each one should have a chance to be all they can become, and she has helped many to succeed in spite of their obstacles and fears. Her wisdom is her strength that propels her forward. She has never been known to lose courage—despite continuous obstacles. The rejection of her gender and color could not stop her. Hattie knew how to move every mountain out of her way and taught her students to do the same. She said, "Never give up in adversity—it's just another step to take you higher."

Hattie said she always believed "you're here to make your mark." Her small beginnings to sponsor and help educate an African child later became a catalyst for improving hundreds of thousands of children's lives in Ghana. Through her fundraising outreach, she was able to help build a school and a clinic in the village of Bomma; now, with continued donations, a library is being built. She joined the Global Association for Health Development Organization and was part of the initiative to dig a well so the community could have clean drinking water. She has been honored by the International Women's Leadership Association for her contributions overseas. Hattie is a member of the Nursing Sorority Chi Eta Phi.

Hattie has become an authentic leader. Throughout her nursing career she has consistently helped nurses reach their full potential. Her positive attitude and loving support have helped many young girls have the courage to remain in the nursing program. She is a courageous role model and teacher. Although Hattie is small in stature, she has become a giant to many—and she has done so by leading with kindness and generosity. Hattie has surely made her mark—not only in nursing but also with multitudes in Ghana.

Debbie: A Hand of Steel in a Velvet Glove

When Debbie considers her career, she recalls those who helped prepare her for the success she never dreamed would come.

The first were her parents, Joseph and Mary. Debbie had a close relationship with her parents. She loved her father's warm, gentle, loving ways. He was a generous man who always did good deeds, but his modesty kept them a secret from most. Her mother, Mary, was a tough disciplinarian whom Debbie admired for her strength and confidence. Debbie's many accomplishments made them so proud of her; they treasured the award ceremonies and newspaper articles. It appears she gleaned the best qualities of them both.

Another person who helped her was Abdullah S. Mishrick, MD. He was Lebanese born and had a long and distinguished relationship with North Shore–LIJ starting in the late fifties—when he did part of his surgical training there. He practiced there for forty years before he was appointed senior vice president for medical affairs at Syosset in 1997; shortly after, he was appointed to the Board of Trustees. Debbie's twenty-year association with him made him a great mentor and friend. She also enjoyed an active friendship with his wife, Jacqueline, for many years. Mishrick's wisdom and guidance helped Debbie win the New York Senate's Annual Woman of Distinction Award in Albany, New York, in 1997. The event honors exceptional achievement, personal excellence, and outstanding courageous actions on the part of individual women from across the state.

A third person that Debbie so loved and admired was her mentor and boss, Michael Dowling, president and CEO of North Shore Health System in New York. In the early years of their relationship, it became apparent to many that their distinct similarities of personality would develop into a close relationship. Dowling liked Debbie's leadership qualities so much that in 1997 he held a special board meeting in which a decision was made to make Debbie the first nurse ever appointed to an executive director position at Syosset hospital. His trust and confidence in her grew as her ability to lead increased exponentially. She created a blueprint for success at Syosset and was then given an opportunity to make it work at a second hospital, Plainview, which she did with equal success. Dowling expanded her authority so she could govern a third hospital, Franklin, and then a fourth, Southside. Over the next ten years, Debbie's blueprint became a model for other hospitals to follow. Dowling's implicit trust in her convinced him to extend her outreach; Debbie became the first nurse to receive the title of regional executive director of six hospitals in the eastern region of Long Island. Debbie retired in the summer of 2012. Dowling created the first nursing scholarship in Debbie's name.

During a very special interview, her sister Jane said that if she could describe Debbie in a few words, they would be "totally selfless." Jane believes Debbie has a giving capacity beyond the ordinary and believes she developed this during their childhood years. When Jane was seven years old, she had open-heart surgery and spent three weeks in the hospital. Looking back, she believed that was a very difficult time for Debbie. She was not allowed to visit her in the hospital, so one day she stood outside the hospital window, and they got to wave to each other. Jane recalls how Debbie always looked out for her— even though she herself was only ten years old. Jane disclosed that if she had to guess (although they never discussed this), she thought that her childhood illness helped shape Debbie's interest in a nursing career. Debbie's "RN" is the title she is most proud of—and what a wonderful nurse she is.

As Jane reminisced about growing up, she recalled that Debbie was a mediocre student in high school but that she really blossomed in college. Once she set her career goal, there was no stopping her. In her senior year of nursing school, Debbie was diagnosed with a torn retina before finals. The surgery needed to be done immediately in order to preserve the vision in her eye. Debbie somehow managed to have the surgery, study, and take her finals. It was so remarkable that when her name was called at graduation, she received a standing ovation. She chose to continue her education after nursing school and earned both a bachelor's degree and a master of science in nursing while caring for two young children, her work, and whoever needed help. Although it was a tremendous undertaking, Debbie made it seem easy.

Although Debbie doesn't attend church, she lives the example of Jesus every day, and he is very real to her. Her life's work—perhaps *joy* is a better word—is to help others. One example of this was when the AIDS crisis first came to light, when Debbie was working at Hempstead General Hospital. At the time, most people, even health-care professionals, feared and shied away. She had a patient who was diagnosed with AIDS and did not have family support; he didn't even have a place to live. Somehow, Debbie found him an apartment and then purchased items to help set him up. She didn't stop there; she also helped him move in. In true Debbie style, however, she didn't believe she had done anything special. In fact, it took a while before anyone even knew what she had done. It was with that same compassion that she continued her career, always putting people first.

Jane smiled as she shared how proud she was to have Debbie for a sister: "Wherever I go, whenever someone realizes that I'm Debbie's sister, the comments are always the same. Consistently and through the many years, people of great diversity share the same view of Debbie: 'Wonderful.' 'What a great person.' 'She helped me so much.' 'So fair.' 'I love her.' 'You are so lucky to have her as a sister.' She's the only person I know who treats every person she meets with the same dignity, equality, and respect, be it the CEO or the housekeeper. To know Debbie and be caught in her embrace is to know true goodness. If anyone has a sick family member, a pot of meatballs is at their door. If there was a crisis in one's life, she sent a thoughtful gift. She always used kind words of encouragement. Throughout my life and through my experiences with others, we all know that Debbie has the ability to take any adversity and make it all better. In our family, she is the first person called if there's a problem. She comforts and reassures and leaves you feeling everything will be just fine—*Debbie said so.* Debbie is fun. Although she has achieved a high level of success, she has not changed. She does not have an ounce of conceit or arrogance in her body. She can go from the boardroom to the dance floor (she does a mean chicken dance) and she's just herself. The party can't officially start until Debbie arrives. I realize every day how lucky I am to have Debbie as my sister. Through the years, she is the thread that is woven into every good thing that has happened in my life. And when things are not so good, she is always my anchor, giving me the courage and confidence to deal with life head on."

Jane ended her time of sharing by saying that Debbie has been an incredible inspiration to her and that she only hopes she can offer Debbie half of what she has received through the years. She expressed her love and gratitude and her pride to be able to call her "sister."

Pat Johnson has been Debbie's secretary for the past thirteen years. She always remembers their first meeting in the administrative office of Plainview hospital. She described Debbie as bubbly and energetic, with a bright smile. Debbie had so many wonderful characteristics—like the many colors of the rainbow—it left Pat speechless. "Hi, Pat, I'm Debbie—let's put this place together!" she recalled Debbie saying. "It was quite a ride. Debbie took all those who were willing to dedicate themselves to her vision and their work to make a difference for the patients at our hospital. We were so proud to be on her team."

Pat considers Debbie to be a compassionate, loving woman. Her zeal and nurturing qualities take her daily to patients' bedsides, where she can be found holding their hands and comforting their families. Her everyday actions are a gift to all those around her. Debbie has a special ability to share herself with all the employees. She knows everyone by name from the administrative staff to the ancillary staff, and she lets it be known that everyone is equally important to the mission. She holds a strong commitment for everyone to advance their education; she believes it will make them better people. Whenever she finds an inspiring quote she always shares it. She even shares her food; her Italian heritage makes her a fabulous cook, and her warm, generous spirit makes her love sharing her food with the staff. Pat sums it up this way: "She is brilliant, funny, and loving . . . She is our Debbie."

"When you are touched by an angel, you may not realize it at that moment. But as time goes by and certain circumstances happen, you begin to realize *this has not happened by coincidence . . . there is an element of the divine.*" This was Noreen Rattler's first impression of Debbie. Noreen went back some fifteen years ago, when she had been hired for a secretarial position for Dr. Abdullah S. Mishrick; she described him as an extraordinarily dedicated and brilliant surgeon at Syosset hospital. Noreen had worked with him in his private practice elsewhere, and she was thrilled to come on board.

Dr. Mishrick joined North Shore in Manhasset in 1967 and remained in the system for thirty-nine years. He spoke over ten languages fluently and always made it seem easy to do. He loved to make people laugh, and he could tell jokes for hours at a time. One of his favorite sayings was, "If you love your job, you won't work a day in your life." Noreen didn't feel like she worked at all.

Noreen thought back to the first time she met Debbie. It was when Dr. Mishrick asked her to pick up lunch. He wanted the order to be *just so*—extra mayonnaise, hero bread cut out. He didn't care about saving the calories; he just wanted it to be delicious, as he was hosting lunch that day with someone very special. Noreen said, "I will always remember when the 'very special' Debbie walked in the room. Her smile lit up the room. Her personality came in the room before she did." Noreen could hear her down the hall talking to the employees: "Hello, how is your day going?" or "Jennifer, how's your mom feeling?" She later learned that Debbie did this on a daily basis. Noreen describes her as a humanitarian with class and grace—and very hard working. Debbie won the favor of Dr. Mishrick; she was grateful for his wisdom and counsel in her career. They worked many long hours and attended many long meetings. They developed a very close friendship—some say it was like a marriage. Dr. Mishrick and Debbie—she was his "Debscha," and he was her "Mishka"

Debbie's unconditional compassion and generosity always amazed Noreen—whether it was giving her time or making meals for those in need. One of her favorite stories was about an employee escort named Maurice; it's a touching account of how Debbie helped his family after he passed away from abdominal cancer. Her gracious generosity gathered together a Christmas tree, presents for the children, and Christmas dinner for the family. Debbie so appreciated how Maurice treated the patients not only in the hospital but also as they left—by escorting them with an umbrella in torrential rain and snow. Noreen could recall at least fifty more stories of Debbie's generosity and kindness to others. "This is merely the tip of the iceberg," she shared. "I have been fortunate to have met an angel named Debbie."

When I met with Debbie's dear friend and colleague Harriet Foreman, her first words to describe Debbie were "Debbie is a hand of steel in a velvet glove." Harriet recalled the time many years ago when she needed an effective nursing management team to help her reverse lackluster, uninspired, and unacceptable care to both acute and long-term care patients. She spotted a staff RN with minimum qualifications. "She worked part-time, and I was told she had resisted all efforts to encourage her to return to school to complete her master's degree—a requirement for the new management team," Harriet explained. "However, her clinical skills were reported as excellent. She was empathetic in human relations, and her outlook on life and on nursing was assertive, courageous, and confident."

As the newly appointed director of nursing, Harriet decided to approach Debbie herself—to discuss a promotion to management. Debbie's first response was "I don't want to be a manager," and then she insisted that she didn't want to return to school. After much ado and many compromises, Debbie joined the management team. She never really left the bedside, however, and Harriet says this is still true of her to this day. Debbie's heart remains with her patients. As her sphere of influence has expanded, she has been able to reach out with her unique ability to know what people need in order to do their jobs.

Harriet shared her joy at watching Debbie grow, develop her skills, her human relations expertise and, yes—her power base—over many years. "Other people in her position might have lost their humility" Harriet explained. "They might have forgotten from where they came. Debbie has not. Underneath the pomp and ceremony, the certificates of achievement, the titles and designations—Debbie is still Debbie, and the world's a better place because Debbie resides in this world."

Debbie's boss, Michael J. Dowling—president and CEO of the North Shore Health System in Long Island, New York—graciously put his thoughts about Debbie on paper:

> Every so often, during the course of your life or your career, you have the privilege and good fortune to interact with a rare species of human being—one who is competent, caring, spiritual, innovative, positive and a change agent and catalyst. This is Debbie Tascone. I have a very clear picture of our first encounter. It was in the mid-1990s. We were in the beginning stages of building the North Shore–LIJ Health System and searching for leaders, not just managers. Believing that observation is an important part of the selection process, I spent time observing the interactions of staff at Syosset Hospital—a new addition to the Health System and in need of leadership. I noticed something unique. Despite having no overall official and formal title or authority, whenever Debbie spoke, everyone listened. She influenced discussions and outcomes by her presence, power of personality, logical thinking, and above all, her passion—the key ingredients of leadership. She was strong-willed yet humble, forceful yet sensitive, opinionated yet engaging and respected. I saw leadership in action, and shortly she became the leader of the hospital. She transformed the facility from being a has-been to a

future beacon of accomplishment—bringing success to be the template for others within the System.

Her roles expanded over time, and Debbie became a key leader of the System as a whole. She was enormously admired by her peers and especially by front line staff. Whenever there was a seemingly intractable problem to solve, the answer invariably was 'call Debbie.'

Debbie lights up whatever space she occupies—a beacon of hope, positivity and optimism. She tackles issues head on, never shrinking from responsibility or accountability. Everyone she has ever touched she has made better, and the field of health care and the NS-LIJ System are eternally grateful.

Her commitment to patients was extraordinary. That, above everything else, is what enshrines her in the memories of those who worked with her. What was good for the patient was, in her view central—the most important thing. And she never wavered.

For me personally, she is an inspiration. A true friend and colleague. Oscar Wilde once stated: "Do not follow where the path may lead; go instead where there is no path and leave a trail."

Debbie not only created one—but many.

I find it difficult to find words that fully define Debbie's remarkable genius. One thing I know is that my heart is filled with gratitude for the many ways she has touched my life. I will never forget how she held my hand and shared my tears when a crisis came to my family. As my boss, she created a new position for me as a holistic nurse—which never existed before. After I graduated from the New York College of Holistic Medicine in 1996, Debbie's innovative ideas began to become a reality. We started with a yearlong pilot study using two holistic therapies with patients: Amma massage therapy and guided imagery (meditation). Debbie's plan was that we would put a proposal together and present it to the medical board members of Syosset and Plainview hospitals. Getting all the doctors to buy into complementary integrative Medicine was something only Debbie could do. In spring of 2001, the Complementary Integrative Medicine Program was born.

I have seen many leaders come and go but few *authentic* leaders. Debbie is a true authentic leader because she has the rare capacity to help people reach their full potential. While most people build their own empires, Debbie builds others' empires. She is a shaker, a mover—nothing and no one remains the same after her touch. She strengthens and inspires; she sees your talents and then makes room for you to grow. She lifts your soul and finds your worth. Debbie makes you feel like the world is a better place because you're in it. She brings heaven wherever she goes. There is no place too high or too low for Debbie; she fears neither. Someone once told me that there is a "Book of Remembrance" in heaven where all our good deeds and acts of kindness are recorded. I'm certain Debbie's book is full.

Irene Fulmer, RN

Michael Left Ireland to Give His Family a Better Life

Within each one of us is a power that when properly grasped and directed can lift us out of the difficult providence in which we find ourselves into a place among the noble of the earth, the thinkers, the doers. Michael Dowling is such a one. He was born in a little village in West Limerick, Ireland, called "Knockaderry." It means "the hill of the mighty oak." It is a long single street village lined with beautiful tall oaks and a large oak grove nearby. The picture this small town portrays is almost prophetic of his life. "Out of a small place will grow a mighty one." With a population of 1,200, life stays simple. Limerick is Ireland's third-largest city and has a beautiful location on one of Ireland's most picturesque rivers, the River Shannon. It is a bustling modern city with the eight-hundred-year-old St. John's Castle, giving it a rich medieval history.

Isn't it always the man who struggles hardest and who gets to the top of the mountain? It was in his youthful age of seventeen, with seemingly insurmountable odds, that Michael was stretched to receive a capacity beyond his years. And in this difficult place he was fitted for the greatness that would follow him in his future work and extraordinary destiny.

During the early 1950s and '60s, much of Ireland was a third-world nation. Living in a thatched roof, three-room cottage with a mud floor and walls made of mud and stone. There was no electricity, no running water, no bathroom, and no heat. Michael recalled, "When you don't know how the rest of the world lives it wasn't so bad because it was all you knew; besides, it toughened you up a bit." Michael's father, John, nicknamed "Jack," suffered from severe arthritis, which ended his role as family breadwinner prematurely at age forty-two and ultimately ended his life at the young age of sixty-one. His mother, Margaret, nicknamed "Meg," became completely deaf after suffering an untoward side effect of a cold remedy. Michael recalls, "My mother had an absolutely fantastic and extraordinary influence on me." She always said, "Never let your circumstances inhibit your potential." She focused on education and challenged her five children to read books. Despite the many hardships in his childhood years, his parents were very loving and supportive. Michael insists that they built a strong solid foundation in him from his youth through their faith in him. "That was the single most invaluable gift they could give me." They were adamant that he receive a full high school education. Today all of his siblings still live in Ireland. His brother, Joe, is a carpenter, and Shawn works for a pharmacy corporation. His sister Mary lives in their hometown, Knockaderry, and Pat is one of the governmental leaders in Limerick City. Michael stays in close relationship with his family via phone conversations every Sunday.

Even though he met the high standard and was top of his graduating class, there was no money for college. Michael persevered in the face of defeat, poverty, and discrimination as he went to Crawley, South London, and worked in a steel factory that summer to support the family. The money he made at the steel mill that summer was enough for his family's provision and his tuition for the 1967 fall semester at University College Cork. He said, "It was a wonderful opportunity. I could see a light at the end of the tunnel. I was thrilled." At seventeen he chose a life devoted to hard work and the selfless caring for and nurturing of his family. Finding a way out of his family's poverty was a pivotal point that later brought much unexpected success. "Try not to become a man of success. Rather become a man of value" Albert Einstein, www.goodreads. com/quotes/tag/albert

The family dreams were beginning to formulate at University College Cork. The beautiful, stately stone buildings with gothic architecture modeled on a typical Oxford college at its center are 178 years old. The college is located in a thriving seaport in the center of town. There is a magnificent coastline by the Atlantic Ocean into great bays, fishing villages, and picturesque harbors. Cork is the largest of all the Irish counties, with rich farmlands, river valleys, and its own international airport. UCC is a world-class university that combines a rich tradition of teaching, research, and scholarship. University College Cork, Ireland. http//www.ucc,ie/en/

A long black gown was required for students to wear in Michael's first and second year "to show they were scholarly," as he said. He was glad the dress code changed to more casual attire for his last two years at UCC. "I remember thinking, *I cannot believe I am here at college.*" In the years that followed, he provided the necessary finances that helped his siblings acquire their education.

In his second year at Cork he spent his summer in America, working long days and even some nights on the waterfront docks in the west side of Manhattan. On his first impression of New York City, he remembers thinking, *My God, I thought I would never get here. How could they build such tall buildings?* He was impressed by the many different faces he saw from all over the world as he walked the city streets. Each fall he returned home to finish his undergraduate degree at UCC, where he also became known as an outstanding hurler, representing his native Limerick's oldest sport.

Michael remains untarnished by materialism. He loves a challenge, and he cares very deeply. He acknowledges the Creator as a reality that influences his life and reflects in a desire to do the right thing. He says it gives him right motives and a desire to help others without self-promotion. This compassion led his path to Fordham University, where he graduated with a master's degree in social welfare. He was considered such a brilliant student that he soon found himself teaching that topic at Fordham, where he quickly climbed the faculty ladder and became a professor. He taught public policy at Lincoln Center and at a Tarrytown campus. While he was teaching at Fordham, he went to Columbia for his doctorate but never submitted his dissertation. Instead, he took a leave of absence from Fordham to accept an invitation from the administration of Mario Cuomo.

In the early 1990s the newly appointed governor of New York, Mario Cuomo, came looking for an innovative mind immersed in social policy to handle the massive health and human services for the state. After some hesitation Michael took the job and stayed for twelve years. It included seven years as state director of health, education, and human services and deputy secretary to the governor. He was appointed commissioner of social services overseeing a thirty-five-million-dollar budget dealing with all the state's welfare, foster care, mental health, substance abuse, and a myriad of other programs. It was a time when focus was on the AIDS crisis and a sudden flood of homeless persons, which he worked to make safe shelters for and get off the streets. He won many awards for his stewardship and showed a particular interest in helping children in need. He developed some very important health-care programs for children during those years. He said, "It was an amazing moment," one he is most proud of—becoming the forerunner for the national Child Health Plus, a major breakthrough in providing health care for children. He said, "If I had the opportunity to have that position again, I would develop a program for childhood obesity." He would address the issues: "what it is that we are suffering from, and what drives the behavior of childhood obesity." He remarked, "More and more people want government to do for them, yet they need to take a corresponding responsibility for themselves."

"For me, this job was the best education you could ever get; it was worth ten doctorates. I was very fortunate. They took a chance with a guy that didn't have very much experience. I found myself in the middle of major issues. They threw things at me, and I loved it. You make mistakes, but you figure out how to fix them. Then you have success. I thoroughly enjoyed working with Governor Cuomo. He is a brilliant, inspiring man who cares deeply; he had an extraordinary influence on me to which I am most grateful."

Today, despite widespread apprehension and uncertainty, there are leaders whose integrity, intelligence, and involvement give us reason to hope. Michael Dowling is such a leader. He acquired the skills set for CEO during the twelve years working with Governor Cuomo. It was right about that time, 1995, that an independent, stand-alone agency, the Long Island North Shore University Hospital, started looking for a director. Michael found himself at the right place at the right time. He was very qualified for the job. Health-care costs spiraling was the world Michael Dowling walked into. He came to North Shore as chief operating officer and played a leading role in the formation of the North Shore–Long Island Jewish Health System. Six years later in 2001 he became its president and CEO. He is one of the most influential CEOs with the third-largest nonprofit in the nation— the largest health system in New York State with a total revenue of more than $7 billion and a total workforce of forty-seven thousand employees, not to mention nine thousand physicians, eleven thousand nurses, and four hundred ambulatory service centers, operating as the single biggest employer on Long Island.

"I'm a risk-taker. I liked that the job wasn't clearly defined." For the first nine months of the job he spent his time developing relationships. "I studied the leaders. I studied those who would lead but were not in leadership positions. I wanted to know what makes them tick and who has the negative influence and who has the positive influence. I learned which buttons you have to push to get the job done. I found if the people don't want to work together, it won't work." Michael was convinced that health care had to change and wanted to be ahead of the curve. He was at the cutting edge of the health-care changes. "I love a challenge. I love competition." The word *impossible* does not exist in his vocabulary. North Shore was out front on this. There was a vague idea, although in its infancy, to merge with other hospitals, hospitals that were once bitter rivals. He immediately built a reputation as a doer, creating a partnership with GE and the Harvard School of Public Health to create the Centre for Learning and Innovation, which is the envy of the medical world. Another one of his successful projects is the Hofstra North Shore–LIJ Medical School.

Michael has demonstrated extraordinary ability to understand and navigate complex issues, such as the merging of sixteen hospitals, while he also strives to best serve the consumers' needs. What's his secret for building a cohesive staff? "It's the secret of reaching compromise," he says. "Spend a lot of time together. You're like a marriage counselor. It is most important to know the organization, the people, their values and behaviors. Find out what interests them; find out about their kids. If you do it right, all the pieces begin to gel. We have had many mergers over the past sixteen years, which have been very interesting and complicated and successful. I never say something can't be done. I always approach things as if there is a solution." He is never afraid to make profound changes when he takes over a new institution as he has recently done with the newly acquired Lennox Hill Hospital. Ray Hughes. ceo radio.com/ interview. May 4, 2013

The world always stands aside for the determined man.

Michael is a remarkably modest man for his accomplishments. He said, "When you believe your press clippings, you lose touch with reality." Some of his many honors include receiving the Distinguished Public Service Award from the State University of New York's Nelson A. Rockefeller College of Public Affairs and Policy, the Alfred E. Smith Award from the American Society for Public Administration, the National Human Relations Award from the American Jewish Committee, and the Ellis Island Medal of Honor. He serves on numerous other boards, including the North American Board of the Smurfit School of Business at University College Dublin, Ireland. In 2011 he was awarded the Gold Medal of the American Irish Society. (http://en.wikipedia.org/wiki/Michael J. Dowling) Regardless of their standing in society, each AIHS Gold Medal recipient has stood out from the crowd not only with outstanding work ethic but also with his or her good nature and outstanding contribution to the history of the Irish people in America. He is also recognized for a life devoted to the selfless caring for and nurturing of others—one of the greatest examples of what Irish grit and determination can do. Michael's seemingly insurmountable climb has surely reached to heaven's gate. He wears the blessings on his shoulders as the proof of the passionate call to those in need and upon whom W. B. Yeats bestowed the eloquent and accurate encomium "the indomitable Irishry." This is Michael Dowling.

Physician's Moment of Epiphany Led to Destiny

Leaders aren't born, they are made. And they are made just like anything else, through hard work. And that's the price we'll have to pay to achieve that goal, or any goal.
—Vince Lombardi

I believe that leadership qualities are part inherent in one's personality and part learned by listening and observing those peers who exhibit examples of leadership qualities.

I was fortunate to have role models of leadership in my family. Both of my grandfathers were immigrants from Europe. They immigrated to the United States, with limited education and funds. They both had a great appreciation and respect for what this country could offer if one possessed tenacity of purpose, a good work ethic, and high moral standards. Through hard work and inner strength, they were both able to build highly successful businesses in the field of couture fashion and luxury leather goods. My grandfather's always took control of their individual situations, and failure was not an option. This life example made an indelible impression on me. My path of accomplishments was guided by their examples of positive direction. Failure to me was not an option. This is the ideology that any leader must embrace.

Another quality embraced by them was to get to know their employees. Through patience and tolerance, they were able to understand their employees' individual goals and to ultimately lead them to exceed their expectations. This inherent, humanistic quality extended to their work staff. You have to impart your trust in people, do the right thing for them, and show them that you have a *human* side. You have to lead with your inner values. You need to make sacrifices when you lead for the overall good of the people, and you need courage and some thinking outside the box to lead successfully.

My parents' message to me was to always know myself and to be able to identify my strengths and weaknesses. They stressed defining what is really important and then accomplishing this with an optimistic drive. Value what is most important and have a meaningful role by impacting people in a positive way—these were principles of quality stressed throughout my upbringing. You have to have this passion in order for quality to become a reality. Superficial rewards are the least important, and one has to make this shift in emphasis to be a true leader. Introspection and self-awareness are values that one needs to have in order to succeed as a leader as well as to overcome new challenges one faces on a daily basis. Confidence in oneself provides a sense of security and thus enables one to communicate effectively and in turn lead. You also must respect others, and they need to respect you so that collectively there is a positive accomplishment.

I recognized the values of consistency and discipline from my teachers, professors, and fellow surgeons. This is not only essential to leadership, but it also engenders approachability of your staff and colleagues. In addition, these same individuals not only inspired me but helped me to attain my goals. This motivation and insight are strong components of leadership that were integral to my successes and ultimate leadership positions. This coupled with a visible confidence is assurance that you are in control.

Another aspect I think is most important to leadership and accomplishing goals is the ability to prioritize and identify significance. It allows one to focus on the real issues. You also need to be happy in your role, and in turn, this will energize you to accomplish progress on a daily basis. Surround yourself with stimulating, intelligent, energetic, and amazing people, and make it your foundation. Add people to this foundation who are dedicated to you and to your vision and can provide a stimulus of enthusiasm to your team members. We need to live our lives for the moment, be energized, dream, and be grateful for the people who come into our lives and for what they offer so as to build character and ultimately solid leadership values.

The question as to why I chose medicine as a career was not a complex decision for me. One of the necessary traits for leadership is to know oneself with regard to one's strengths and weaknesses, as I previously mentioned. My first exposure to a career choice was growing up in a family of businesspeople. During the summers I worked at my grandfather and father's business in the garment industry on 7th Avenue in NYC. They manufactured and designed couture clothes for women. This was a high-end fashion industry with national and international recognition, especially because of their iconic designer Claire McCardell. Examples of her clothing are displayed in many museums across the country, including the Costume Institute in the Metropolitan Museum of Art in New York City. It was indeed very interesting work for me during the summers, but once I got past the glamour aspects and got involved in the real aspects of the business, I realized it was not my passion. It was not the pace of the business but rather my lack of desire to embrace the many nuances of running a successful business. I had the same insight when I worked with my other grandfather in the leather goods industry.

I had other work experiences that exposed me to different aspects of human interaction. These included working for the sanitation department as a garbage collector and serving as a bellhop, movie usher, waterskiing teacher, and horseback-riding instructor at summer camps. These opportunities showed me that I was very comfortable working with individuals from all different backgrounds, and I experienced people looking to me for direction and leadership.

An experience that made me look into medicine was my appreciation and regard for our family physician. In my junior year of college I became quite ill and had to leave school for six months. My illness was quite severe, consisting of liver failure, extreme weakness, high fevers, and significant weight loss. This ultimately was diagnosed as mononucleosis, but since the testing at that time was not that specific, the question of leukemia was not initially ruled out. My family physician came to see me at least two times a day to draw blood, perform an examination, and give me emotional support. When I was watching him and listening to him, I had my epiphany. I wanted to become a physician. He had the qualities of humanism, dedication, intellect, and the ability to achieve significant personal gratification in helping people get their health and lives back to normal. This was a great man who embraced all the qualities that physicians as well as a leader in the community strive for.

The imprinting of such qualities assimilates them into our being and shapes us to a significant degree. This was further evidenced by one of my teachers at the Cleveland Clinic Foundation, where I did my residency training. He was a brilliant and talented young attending surgeon. He was trained at the Mayo Clinic and had the gift of a photographic memory in addition to the gift of expressing himself clearly in his teaching, which effectuated learning. His manner, confidence, and surgical expertise made him a nationally and internationally noted surgical specialist in pancreatic surgery. He became my mentor, and thus, I changed my direction from cardiac surgery to abdominal and digestive surgery. Again, having this privileged opportunity to work with such an accomplished surgeon and individual further promoted the qualities of leadership that are required to be a successful surgeon and leader.

Ultimately because of the aforementioned individuals, who have imprinted my life and the values they imparted to me, I was able to become a very accomplished surgeon. I am the recipient of many awards of recognition and have been admitted to many prestigious medical and surgical societies. I have also received many certificates both locally and nationally, reflecting my surgical expertise and accomplishments.

Another interest that played a significant role in my development as a surgeon and leader was playing sports. I was actively involved in various sports, including baseball, tennis, football, waterskiing, basketball, and golf. All of these are of benefit not only from an exercise point of view but also with regard to developing a sense of integrity, honesty, a competitive attitude, and dealing with failure. I was always told that one cannot succeed with failures. Of all the sports, golf was the most enjoyable to me because of its values. The game is played with the expectation of high morality and honesty. It embraces a competitive attitude and true gamesmanship, which can be applied to other aspects in one's life. One also has to have the fortitude to accept that golf can be "a good walk spoiled," as stated by Mark Twain, and to deal with the inconsistencies, degrees of difficulty, and poor shots that punctuate this game. It is a counterintuitive game. To hit the ball up, you need to hit down on the ball, and to hit the ball far, you need to swing slow. In spite of this and poor scores, people still come back again and again, knowing they can improve. So golf is a metaphor for life and thus a very important virtue to recognize. We *need to fail in order to succeed*. In golf, our strengths and weaknesses will always be there. If one can improve on one's weaknesses, the game would improve. The paradox is that people tend to practice their strengths. Thus, it reinforces what I stated earlier. For one to succeed as a leader, one has to be aware of one's weaknesses and work on improving them for future success. Golf certainly has helped me in this regard!

Leadership qualities are thus not inherent but are learned by our exposures to the various people in our lives. If you are attentive, you will find the virtues and direction in your character that will formulate your own direction as to profession and leadership.

Alan is quite humble for his many outstanding inventions and awards. In 1980 he invented an anti-air embolism device (US Patent #4230109). A few years later he invented a nasogastric tube that was adapted to avoid pressure necrosis (US Patent #4363323). One year later he developed a percutaneous implantable triple lumen catheter. He is a member of the Association of Academic Society and a diplomat of the American Board of Surgery. He is a fellow at the American College of Surgeons and a member of the New York Academy of Medicine. He is a member of the Society of Laparoendoscopic Surgeons and the American Society of Bariatric Surgeons. Alan has received many distinguished honors. In 2000 he appeared in *New York Magazine* as "The Best Doctor in New York," and in the Castle Connolly Guide he was named one of the "Top Doctors New York Metro Area" in 2003and 2008. In 2009, ACC distinguished him as one of the "Top Doctors of Long Island."

An Interview with Visionary Nurse Leader,

Maureen T. White, R.N., MBA, NEA-BC, FAAN,
is the Chief Nurse Executive and Senior Vice President at the
North Shore-LIJ Health System

Lily Thomas: Maureen, I want to begin this interview by thanking you; I am one of the 11,000 nurses who have benefited from your leadership. This is a great opportunity for me and others to understand your vision and thought process. Thank you for granting the interview. What inspired you to become a nurse?

Maureen White: There is no single moment or event that inspired me to become a nurse. It's something I always wanted to do. Even as a child, I was intrigued by and drawn to any kind of shows and movies related to medicine or health care. As I got older and began to study nursing, I found the subject matter increasingly fascinating and the ability to help others compelling. But, there wasn't any particular moment when the light bulb went on; there was just never any doubt that I wanted to be a nurse.

Lily Thomas: What are your favorite memories of your family?

Maureen White: My family is everything to me. So, I have many favorite memories of our time together: going to the beach, going to the museums, holidays, just enjoying our time together.

Lily Thomas: I know you were very close with your mother and she has impacted your life and career. Can you comment on that?

Maureen White: My mother was a great woman; both my parents were dedicated to the family and to making sure that no matter what we did in life, we gave it our best. There were eight children in my family, with an age gap of 18 years between the oldest and the youngest. My mother had to, in her own way, manage the different generations and she did it masterfully. She made all of us believe that we were her only child. She made each of us feel unique and very special. She didn't compare one child to the other. She looked at every one as an individual and looked at the great attributes of each one of us and what our strengths were, not just within the family unit, but what our strength would be in life. She was a great motivating force and inspiration to everyone that knew her. To this day, more than 15 years after her death, I hear stories from people how she touched their lives and will never be forgotten. I remember a young fellow in the local deli that she would always chat with when she was in the store. She always asked him, "What are you doing? Are you in school? How are you doing here in the shop?" She planted the seed in his mind that someday she expected to see him running his own deli. Many years later he reached out to let her know that because of her, he had purchased his own deli. He told her that he would never have thought about it if she had not given him those encouraging words whenever she came into the store. She was a very special person in that way. She was not judgmental. She appreciated and valued each person, always looked for the positive in life, very upbeat, very gregarious, she had the warmest laugh you could ever hope to hear. She was simply magnificent. She instilled in all of her children that the greatest legacy any of us can leave is to help those around us achieve their dreams and aspirations in life and to watch them flourish- that it was not about just what we get out of life, but what were we giving to life -how we could help make a better world for the people around us.

Lily Thomas: That is so great; and you have modeled that in your leadership. What was the greatest lesson you learned from your nursing career and life?

Maureen White: My mother set the bar high and will always be a hard act to follow, but I try my best each day to follow her example. Many times I succeed, sometimes I have to try harder, but the greatest life lesson that nursing has taught me is that every life is precious and too short. There are many silly things we fret over, worry about – that's a waste of valuable time. John Lennon once said that, " life is what happens while you are busy making other plans". I think that too often we make things unnecessarily complex. We have to keep things simple, understand what is and is not important and neither fixate or worry about things over which we have no control. We need to do our best in all things and get on with living while we have the chance.

Life is precious and too short. As nurses, we are very detail oriented which is wonderful, but sometimes I think that we spend too much time on the minutiae and lose sight of the bigger picture. We are so busy trying to make a perfect system -we fail to realize we don't live in a perfect world- and there is seldom such a thing as a perfect system. So we become paralyzed in many respects by over analyzing, over reflecting; trying to make everything perfect instead of moving ahead and seeing where life takes us.

Lily Thomas: Has your vision for nursing become a reality and what is your vision for nursing's future?

Maureen White: My vision for nursing is always evolving, just as the healthcare paradigm is evolving. I believe nurses today, and in the future, need to be knowledgeable, current in their practice, analytical, with a focus on the entire patient and their healthcare needs throughout the continuum of care, not just in their individual silos of care. My vision for nursing is for nurses to be recognized as an important component of the healthcare workforce team and for nurses to appreciate the integral role that they play in the healthcare delivery system. Nurses are – and should see themselves as being – more than -just task masters. We are so much more. We have an analytical side coupled with a deep understanding of human behavior and human needs. It is not just about the task, it is about the caring and compassion that we can give to an individual at their moment of greatest need. I believe very strongly unless you have a high functioning registered nursing staff and nursing care team, you will not have a high quality healthcare team. Creating the environment for nurses to flourish has been my goal and then it is up to each individual nurse to empower themselves to want to achieve those high standards and expectations in their nursing practice. In the future, I see nursing being recognized more for the unique perspective that we bring to the table; the melding of not just the clinical side, but the business and humanistic sides of healthcare. I see nursing playing a larger role than had ever been anticipated decades ago.

Lily Thomas: Thank you. It is said that we are not physical beings having a spiritual experience but we are spiritual beings having a human experience. Can you comment on that?

Maureen White: I was brought up in a family that believed in a higher being. We were very much focused on our religious beliefs. Our religious principles were part of our upbringing and how we conducted ourselves. I do believe in a higher being and I do believe that helps to guide us along our paths in life. I don't know if I can say that we are physical beings having a spiritual experience or that we are spiritual beings having a human experience. I think that everybody believes in different things and there are some people who believe in nothing, but that doesn't mean that they aren't moved by something. So I wouldn't want to characterize it one way or the other. I think we are all moved by something.

Lily Thomas: So, you believe in the existence of the creator, how does it impact your work?

Maureen White: All of life's experiences form who I am. As a result, I consider how my decisions and actions affect others. I believe that every life is intrinsically important and that everyone has the ability to contribute positively at some level and in some way to better the world. Each life should be respected and valued. What is personally important to me and what I try to bring to my work is that I continue to strive to be the best person I can be – that I am able to look in the mirror each day knowing I have tried in every situation to accomplish the best possible result; that I can look back, without regrets; and to treat people as I would want to be treated.

Lily Thomas: How do you spend your down time? How do you relax?

Maureen White: My down time is spent with my family-that is where I am the happiest. It could be a simple cup of tea or a phone conversation with my sisters or brothers, hosting holiday celebrations, or just going to the grocery store for everyday routine items with my nieces or nephews. The most fun I have in life is with my family and it doesn't matter what we do just so long as we are together.

Lily Thomas: Do you have a special cause that you are interested in?

Maureen White: I do, I am very interested in Down syndrome, which is a condition that does not receive sufficient attention even though it is the most commonly occurring chromosomal disorder. Individuals with Down syndrome are absolutely wonderful and make tremendous contributions to their families, communities and society. They also have significant needs, and I am particularly excited by the tremendous recent progress in the area of Down syndrome cognitive research. This work has the potential to positively impact the lives of this very deserving group of people.

Lily Thomas: What does retirement look like?

Maureen White: I don't know. I would have to say retiring probably will involve volunteer services, volunteering in some organization to help others and spending a lot of time with my family.

Lily Thomas: If you could turn the clock back -would you make any changes?

Maureen White: No, I believe things happen in life for reasons. If I changed any of the decisions that I made or the paths that I took, then the course of my life would have changed as well and who knows where that would have taken me. I am a true believer that things happen in our lives for reasons that we don't always understand and this probably goes back to my spiritual side. I think it's a matter of embracing the paths you are on, rising to the occasion, making adjustments as needed, and appreciating and growing from the lessons learned. There is nothing that I would have changed – I believe this was what I was meant to do and the path I was meant to take.

Lily Thomas: When you consider the enormous success that has come in your career, does it surprise you?

Maureen White: Nobody is more surprised than me because it was never in any of my conscious thoughts or game plan that this is where

I would ultimately be. I always saw myself a nurse at the bedside. It is one of those things where circumstances came up, opportunities presented themselves, and I was drawn to different pathways. It was embracing all of those new opportunities and saying I'll give it my best and let's see where it goes. Some of the pathways seemed like logical next steps and some of the pathways seemed more risky and out of my comfort zone. Regardless of which pathway it was, there was always one common element that I brought along with me and that was the patient and putting the patient first.

Lily Thomas: Please share anything else that you think is important.

Maureen White: I think that it's important, in healthcare as in life, to have balance. As important as the work that we do, it is also important to have some down time - to reflect on the work you are doing, to re-energize yourself, to re-focus yourself on where you are going, where you want to go, and where you need to go. You must give yourself time to have those moments of reflection so you can ensure that you are living up to your fullest capabilities. I think we tend to fall into the trap, from time to time, of thinking we are the only one that can solve the problems. We need to stop ourselves from this way of thinking because there are many capable people around us. We are not servicing the patients, the organization, or ourselves if we allow ourselves to get into this spiral of thinking that the weight of the world is on our shoulders; there are many people in this world to share that weight. It is also important to keep your sense of humor. We work in a very serious business, regularly dealing with life and death. This does not mean, however, that we can't smile, enjoy each other's company, and have some fun at work. To the contrary, it is important for each of us and for those around us that we smile and laugh from time to time. We shouldn't always walk around like the world is ending, because it's not. Those are some of the things I have learned over the years.

SPIRITUAL ASCENT

CHAPTER 10

RESTORING NURSING'S SPIRITUAL HERITAGE

A History of Prayer in Nursing

N ursing publications in America began to proliferate in the early twentieth century. Nightingale—being the forerunner—wrote a number of articles about the importance of prayer in the life of the nurse. One example is an article published in the *Public Health Nurse* of June 1923, in which the author asserted that "all who embrace nursing as a life profession must have as a secret source of their ministering contacts" a prayerful relationship with God. And a 1926 commentary in *The Trained Nurse and Hospital Review* suggested that nurses approach a bedside from a posture of prayer. The author of a 1937 textbook, *The Art and Science of Nursing*, advised that the nurse offer a patient a form of a spiritual therapy—such as reading from the bible or saying a prayer. In 1939, a prayer—composed for the graduation ceremony of a nursing school—asked the nurses to heal broken hearts and soothe disquieted minds with the balm obtained from the celestial pharmacy, which strengthens, comforts, sheers and cures. In 1954 "Night Nurse's Prayer," published in *The Catholic Nurse*, included the concept of seeing Christ in all of one's patients: "I looked at my patient there in the bed, but I felt I was seeing the thorn-crowned head."

As to contemporary publications in nursing, many fundamental texts include some reference to prayer as a dimension of the nurse's practice. A literature search to identify journal articles—one focused on the relationship between nursing and prayer—revealed thirty-four publications from 1989 to 2000. A search for prayer as a key concept in nursing journal articles under such headings as "spiritual care," "nursing care," "spirituality," "nurse-patient relations," and "ethics," however, identified 21,319 items.

In the 1990s, a number of nursing publications identified gentleness as an undergirding theme of nursing. "Gentle Persuasion" (Keachie 1992) was recommended in 1992 as the best way to approach an isolated patient. A 1993 article spoke of the importance of compassionate and gentle handling of chronically ill patients; a 1997 ethnographic study described nurses' openness as reflected in the use of a gentle touch, and a 1998 qualitative study of chronically ill children found that the children's coping was notably strengthened by the gentle caring of their nurses (O'Brien 2003).

Overview: Nursing Research on Spiritual Care

Much has been achieved in the last fifteen years, evidenced by the increase in spiritual care policy and the proliferation of writing, debate, and research in the area of spirituality and health. A fifteen-year review of nursing research on spiritual care from 1983 to 2005 was initiated by Linda Ross, senior lecturer for the School of Care Sciences at the University of Glamorgan in South Wales. In one of the earliest studies it was indicated that nurses had very limited awareness of patients' spiritual needs (Highfield and Carson 1983).

It is encouraging that more recent studies show that on the whole nurses were quite good at identifying and assessing spiritual needs.

There were fourteen studies on nurses. Half of these were conducted in the United Kingdom, the highest proportion in the oncology/hospice setting. The focus of these studies was on describing and exploring nurses' perceptions and awareness of patient/client/caregiver spiritual needs and their responses to these needs. Most studies found that nurses' definitions/perceptions of spiritual need reflected the broad range found in the literature but that they tended to focus on religious needs (Narayanasamy 1993, Ross 1994, Harrington 1995, Taylor et al. 1995, McSherry 1998, Carroll 2001, Narayanasamy et al. 2002). In one study (Strang et al. 2002) nurses held a more existential view of spiritual needs, and in some studies nurses reported difficulty in defining the concept (Ross 1994, Harrington 1995, Strang et al. 2002). Although nurses acknowledged that spiritual care was part of their role and expressed a willingness to be involved, it seems that in reality they responded less well. They frequently did not respond at all or did so on an ad hoc basis (Narayanasamy 1993, Ross 1994, McSherry 1998, Kuuppelomaki 2001, Stranahan 2001). Most studies attributed this to nurses feeling inadequately prepared to give spiritual care.

A number of studies identified factors that appeared to influence if and how spiritual care was given by nurses. The findings are fairly consistent and suggest that spiritual care is promoted where nurses are aware of their own spirituality, e.g., beliefs and life experience (Boutell and Bozer 1990, Ross 1994, Harrington 1995, Taylor et al. 1995, Carroll 2001, Kuuppelomaki 2001, Stranahan 2001, Narayanasamy et al. 2002); good links with other professionals, such as chaplains and clergy (Ross 1994, Kuuppelomaki 2001); and the environment is conducive, e.g., adequate staffing, time, and/or resources (Boutell and Bozett 1990, Ross 1994, Harrington 1995, McSherry 1998, Carroll 2001). Nurses have been educated in spiritual care (Harrington 1995, Taylor et al. 1995, McSherry 1998, Carroll 2001, Lundmark 2005). Patients are in a position to communicate their needs to staff (Boutell and Bozett 1990, Ross 1994, Kuuppelomaki 2001).

There were twenty-three studies that focused on patient/clients/caregivers. The majority was conducted in North America in an oncology/hospice setting. The main focus of the studies was exploration of the meaning of spirituality and spiritual need, spiritual care, and spiritual coping/growth and exploring the relationships between the variables.

While some patients/clients/caregivers expressed difficulty in defining or articulating spirituality and spiritual need (Taylor 2003), most acknowledged the spiritual dimension was an important part of their lives, providing a source of strength, hope, and well-being, especially during illness, loss, and/or hospitalization (Simsen 1988, Conco 1995, Narayanasamy 1995, Watson 1999, Cavendish et al. 2000). People's descriptions of the spiritual dimension and spiritual needs/sources of support were wide-ranging but usually included a vertical/metaphysical/transcendent element and a horizontal/existential element (Simen 1986, Walton 1999, Lowry and Conco 2002, Taylor 2003, Murray et al. 2004, Narayanasamy 2004). Ross concludes that more research needs to be done and should be done in conjunction with policy makers at both government and professional levels, if spiritual care is to be given its rightful place.

Doing God's Work

Entrust your works to the Lord, and your plans will succeed.
—Proverbs 16:3 GWT

This quality of spiritual virtue in the nursing profession is the very core and heart of God, and it is by his grace and favor that it is given. The foundation of nursing is of eternal value because it bears the marks of the Creator and his ownership of it. Jesus said, "I was sick and you cared for me; I was hungry and you gave me food; I was thirsty and you gave me a drink." The disciples asked him, "When did we do these things?" Jesus answered, "When you did them to even the least of them, your brothers, you did it unto me" (www.heartlight.org). God always agrees with what is like him, what is like his nature; his nature is love and compassion. He has always demonstrated his favor toward nurses' commitment and devotion in the ministry of caring for the sick. Florence Nightingale was the forerunner of such pure devotion and today is still thought of as a "ministering angel" to the sick. Nightingale said, "Nursing is doing God's work, it is a service to God's most fragile and most needy and that is the charisma, the spiritual capacity given by God's grace to be used for the benefit of others. That is the gift of nursing."

Victorian hierarchical religious and militaristic models of instruction also influenced Nightingale's nursing theory and ethics. For Nightingale, nursing was a spiritual calling of an inclusive character, requiring a total commitment of body, mind, and soul. Nurses had to see a patient as a person in a holistic sense, with intellectual, emotional, social, and spiritual components, one that the nurse was required to form a relationship with. The interpersonal and reciprocal relationship that a nurse had with a patient was the essence of nursing practice for Nightingale. She felt that nursing was a self-defining moral and religious practice. In the early days nursing was only open to those who felt a deep-seated altruism that led them to dedicate their entire lives to aiding humanity. As Nightingale states, "But more than this, she must be a religious and devoted woman; she must have respect for her own calling, for God's precious gift of life is often literally placed in her hands. It was for this reason that not any woman could be a nurse, but only a woman who had a virtuous character."

To understand why a nurse's morality was so important, it is helpful to highlight Nightingale's notion of disease. Nightingale understood disease as an expression of the deviation of the patient from nature—nature, she understood, as being the expression of God's supreme will. Disease was due to the fact that fresh air, light, warmth, cleanliness, quiet, and a proper diet were needed by the patient. Hence, disease was a restorative process of the patient trying to regain a lost union with God's will by returning to a natural as well as ethical harmony. All nursing could accomplish—and it was no small achievement—was to put the patient into the best possible condition for nature to affect its plan of cure. By aiding the patient to restore this union with God's will, the nurse was not only acting on a patient's physiology but also aiding a patient ethically and spiritually.

It was very different than today. The spiritual and ethical virtues of a nurse took hierarchical priority, the practical skills coming second and the intellectual skills last. Comments about nurses in both hospital records and the nursing press of the time draw attention to Nightingale's idea that a nurse's character was more important than theoretical knowledge and more important even than education.

Nightingale called it a sacred commission given to nurses. She acknowledged that it would require the grace of prayer and spiritual growth for nurses to be faithful to this calling. And yet, in this era of health-care reform, of managed care and restructured nursing roles, what does prayer mean for the contemporary nurse? How can nurses find the time for prayer in a caregiving system in which all activities must be cost effective and time efficient?

It appears that an awakening to the spiritual importance in caring for the sick is already underway, because in the last decade the Joint Commission (TJC) has recognized the importance of spiritual and religious beliefs and traditions for persons who are ill or disabled. This concern is reflected in the TJC standards relating to spiritual assessment and spiritual care—both for those who are hospitalized and those living in nursing homes. These standards are now bringing awareness and resources that help meet the spiritual needs of the patient.

The word *compassion* is defined as "a feeling of deep sympathy for another's distress or for one who is stricken with illness." It's accompanied by a strong desire to alleviate the suffering. Its Latin root means "to suffer" with someone, to take the pain of their burden. The nursing literature on compassion supports that understanding, with articles on topics such as compassionate caring, compassion for suffering, and empathy/compassion. Prayer is just one of the many ways to express compassion in nursing. In prayer, although we are petitioning God, we are also focusing on the development of a personal relationship with God.

> *Prayer is opening our understanding to God's brightness and light, and exposing our will to the warmth of His love. . . . It is a spring of blessings and its waters quench the thirst of the passions of our heart, wash away our imperfections, and make the plants of our good desires grow green and bear flowers.*—St. Francis De Sales

In today's complex and stressful health-care environment, prayer provides the ability to truly embrace patients' needs and truly practice compassionate caregiving. The answer is nursing. In the midst of her crowded unit, the nurse can enter the innermost garden of her soul and dwell alone with God—in the solitude where the two meet. In the midst of all the noise of her work, she can retreat to a place of silence where she can listen to the still, small voice within. She can practice this by finding ways to be alone during her time off away from all the chatter and noise. Here she can rest, observe, listen, or journal. In this drawing aside, she can rid herself of the contamination of the soul that accrues from constant interaction with others and the world around us. Wordsworth's poem says it well: "the world is too much with us." He loved nature and found his solitude walking in wooded trails. Nurses can find this unique place of quiet communion, not so much from head knowledge but from heart understanding. She can discover her soul and nurture her inner being. Acknowledging and achieving this inner quiet is not easy, yet silence is the core of all prayer. In the beginning stages, we often hear our own inner voice much louder than God's voice. Slowly, however, we discover that the silence leads to prayer. And once again we experience the presence of God speaking to and interacting with us. Once we have found the inner sanctuary, this special place of silence, we become eager to find it again. Practicing His presence regularly will bring favorable benefits.

The implication that cognitive abilities and our five senses are important for an understanding of God and thus a relationship with Him is evidenced through such scripture as Isaiah 1:18 where the invitation is given by the Lord to Isaiah to reason together with Him. Further scripture supports the use of cognitive perception and the senses "let him who has ears to hear let him hear" (Matthew 11:15. The writer of Ecclesiastes (8:17) speaks of wise men saying they know; but are not able to discover the truth. Time spent in meditation can give you unbelievable strength and power for the daily routine of living.

I have formulated three keys to caring to assist you in demonstrating Nightingale's care of the soul. If you choose to use these prayers as part of your nursing practice, it will help you create an atmosphere for nurturing and healing and promote your own spiritual growth.

Three Keys to Caring

Key 1. Set Your Intention

Each day, dedicate your work to God for the benefit of each patient and coworker. Since compassion is the key to all healing, demonstrate compassion in your actions. Set your intention for the patient's highest good.

Key 2. Initiate Presence

Be still, quiet your mind, and take a slow, deep breath. Center yourself in your spirit by acknowledging your union with the Creator before you go to each patient. Acknowledge that God is in you and works through you.

Key 3. Make Contact

Always make eye contact with your patient. Honor the patient, knowing that he or she is made in the Creator's image. Make sure you convey empathy in your voice and show compassion through a smile or a gentle touch. Offer love in your attitude. Express gratitude for the holy work you are doing.

The great apostle Paul spoke of God's gift of the Holy Spirit and the gifts that accompany it for the care of the sick. He said in Hebrews 2:4 that the evidence that God was with us was in his giving of the Holy Spirit and the various gifts. There are different kinds of spiritual gifts or special endowments of supernatural energy of the Holy Spirit—but the same spirit. There are different forms of service and ministration, but it is the same God. These gifts are distinctive varieties and distributions of extraordinary powers due to the divine grace operating in the soul by the Holy Spirit. To one is given the power to speak a message of wisdom; to another, a word of knowledge. To another, the gift is the wonder working faith; to another, it's extraordinary powers of healing. Someone might have the gift of working miracles; someone else might have prophetic insight, the gift of interpreting the divine will and purpose of God. To another, the gift might be the ability to discern and distinguish between the true spirit and false ones. Another might have the ability to speak in a heavenly language; yet another might have the ability to interpret it. All these gifts and abilities are inspired and brought to fruition by the Holy Spirit (1 Corinthians 12:12 AV).

Brother Lawrence was born in the early 1600s. He served for fifteen years in a Carmelite monastery in Paris as the community cook, and he is sometimes referred to as "the saint of the pots and pans." He is remembered for the intimacy he expressed concerning his relationship to God and for his ability to practice awareness of the presence of God in his daily activities. He gained popularity for his ability to bring the presence of God into his work environment. Brother Lawrence learned the power of silence and its calming effect on the mind and heart; he discovered that silence makes the right atmosphere for prayer. Perhaps the greatest of men are those who never seek greatness at all but who personify the virtues which posterity calls great. Despite his lowly position in life, his godly character attracted many to him. He had a reputation for experiencing the profound presence of God and visitors came to seek spiritual guidance from the great wisdom he carried. The wisdom he passed on to many, in conversations and in letters, would later become the basis for *The Practice of the Presence of God*. This book became especially popular among Catholics and Protestants. Great leaders of the faith, such as John Wesley and A. W. Tozer, highly esteemed his teachings and recommended the book to others. Lawrence said, "Silence is not a thing outside of us but an ineffable presence that calls us to prayer" (Lawrence 1967). It is these brief moments of reflecting on the awareness of God's presence in our lives that will inform and bless the nurse and allow nurses to truly become contemplative caregivers.

> *Lord of all pots and pans and things . . . make me a saint by getting meals and washing up the plates.*—Brother Lawrence (1967)

Are all nurses called to a degree of mysticism in their work? John Welch, a member of the Carmelites, defines mysticism as "a loving knowledge of God which is born in a personal encounter" and which results in "a life which is built upon one's direct experience of God." He adds, "Today, mysticism is viewed as a common and normal activity, although often implicit, in the lives of all Christians." As a member of the Carmelites, Welch discloses, "Geographically, we take our name from Mount Carmel, a green oasis in Israel surrounded by desert. *Carmel* in Hebrew means *Garden of God*. Metaphorically, Carmel is our spiritual disposition as we climb higher in our journey of faith." Having an attitude of deep reverence toward God and one's fellow human beings is a fundamental sign of genuine mysticism.

Karl Rahner was one of the most influential German Catholic theologians of the twentieth century. He believed that each of us is called to be "at least an anonymous mystic." In his book *Mystic of*

Everyday Life, he contended that even everyday life could be holy. He said, "Whenever there is radical self-forgetting for the sake of the other, there is the mysticism of everyday life." His understanding of mysticism supports the appropriateness of the call of every nurse to becoming a mystic. In nursing we have so many opportunities to encounter the divine in the continuous cycles of death and birth, of illness and recovery, of suffering and healing. Nurses can experience "the mystic within" our own spirits and discover the mysticism in our everyday nursing practice.

Gentleness: A Spiritual Intervention

Mary Elizabeth O'Brien, author of the book, *Prayer in Nursing,* asked a group of nurses to share their thoughts and experiences with gentleness in their practice of nursing.

An oncology nurse provided a definition of spiritual gentleness:

> Spiritual gentleness is a quality shown by the nurse who believes she has been called to care for others by the way scripture teaches; kindly, nonjudgmentally, and with a soft touch . . . the nurse believing she is "called" is important because it influences how she cares. It is possible that gentleness can be automatic, though admirable, action. The qualifier, *spiritual,* means that the nurse is actively thinking, living, spiritually, and even praying, while she is acting.

Another adult nurse practitioner highlighted the relationship of spiritual gentleness to caring.

> Spiritual gentleness is intertwined with the concept of caring as the core of the nursing model. The word *spiritual* can have meaning that extends along a continuum. For example, it can be considered that caring itself is a spiritual act. On the other end of the continuum is when

the nurse directly prays with a patient. Some possible synonyms for spiritual gentleness are spiritual sensitivity, caring, empathy, compassion, or healing touch. A nurse manager and patient educator identified three specific characteristics of spiritual gentleness: spiritual gentleness evokes feelings of understanding and acceptance—it is rooted in the frailty of our humanness; spiritual gentleness increases peace and harmony; spiritual gentleness is the basic ingredient of love.

Lastly, a male nurse working with life-threatening illness commented:

I personally see spiritual gentleness in nursing as a way to reconnect with my own feelings/beliefs about spirituality and my commitment to the nursing profession. Spiritual gentleness assists me with my own fears about death and dying and helps me cope with working with patients who have a life-threatening chronic disease.

When God Visits Us: Inspirational True Stories

God comes to us as the sick, the lonely, the poor, and the dying. Do we recognize him when he comes?

The nurse on 3 West asked me to see the patient in room 366. She said, "The patient is a forty-six-year-old with a diagnosis of end-stage ovarian cancer." When I met Gladys she was very receptive to my holistic therapy services and wanted to experience them for herself. Gladys had much to say during our daily visits together. She enjoyed sharing about her childhood years living in a convent with nuns and about her loving memories of them. Although Gladys had a deep faith and love for God, one day during my visit with her she asked me "Why has God forgotten me?" Her faith was being shaken by her long illness and intense pain. Without trying to force an answer to such a difficult and unexpected question, I just spontaneously answered "God hasn't forgotten you," and I shared a scripture about God's omnipresence and that he even watches over a tiny sparrow—he knows when they fall to the ground. I said, "Aren't you of more value than the sparrow? God not only sees but understands everything about you." The words seemed to comfort her. "Can we pray?" she asked. After our prayer together, Gladys asked if I smelled the roses. She said there was a beautiful scent of roses all over the room, yet there were no roses or other flowers in the room. Gladys was enjoying the smell of roses; she believed God had given this to her as a sign of his love and favor toward her. All her doubts were gone. I told her I didn't smell the roses, but I was certain that she did because God had come to visit Gladys that day. I knew when I left her that I would not see her again, that when I would return after a long Labor day weekend, her bed would be empty—she would have left this world the day before. It happened just as I intuitively knew. When I went to her room that day after the holiday, her bed was empty. The nurse said, "Oh, didn't you know? Gladys died yesterday." I said to myself, *Yes, just as I saw it.*

Several years ago I received a call from the emergency room supervisor asking if I could see a twenty-seven-year-old who was being readmitted with end-stage stomach cancer. When I got to Paul's room, his mother and brother practically knocked me over to get out of the room. I thought, *How could they leave him at this time when he needs them the most?* As quickly as the question came, the answer followed: *They can't cope with Paul's illness; they're afraid he is dying and they don't know what to do.* I introduced myself to Paul and a deep dialogue quickly followed. Paul said, "I'm too young to die—I want to get married and have a family, and I'm too young to die." It was an emotional moment, and I knew I needed wisdom to respond to Paul's frustrations and anxieties. I answered, "You're right, Paul, you *are* too young to die." My agreement with him seemed to calm him, and he said, "My father died a year ago, and I don't want to die. Do you think God could heal me?" Paul opened a door when he spoke about God, so I answered him on that level of faith. I told him I believed that he could be healed. He said he was Catholic, so I pursued his belief in the resurrection and life after death. Throughout the conversation, Paul held my hand and continuously told me he loved me, to which I responded back each time, "I love you too, Paul." We discussed his faith and the promises that were his regarding eternal life. I told Paul I believed that if God were going to heal him, every cell in his body would be made completely whole and he would be healed. If God were taking him to his eternal home, he would go to a far better place than his home on earth. Paul asked me to read the scriptures; he wanted to hear the twenty-third psalm. I recited the Amplified version:

The Lord is my shepherd, I have everything that I need, He lets me walk in meadows green and he leads me beside the quiet streams, he keeps on giving life to me and he helps me to do what honors him the most, even when walking through the dark valley of death, I will never be afraid for he is close beside me.

While we were talking that afternoon, I knew intuitively that Paul's father would be coming for him very soon to take him home; I quietly pondered this. Paul moved from a place of great resistance to a calm acceptance and peace. I was certain of God's intervention and his great grace in our conversation. I was grateful for the wisdom that flowed and the strong presence of God's spirit that came to comfort Paul. I learned a lot that day. I learned the importance of *compassion* and being able to share Paul's emotional pain during his spiritual crisis. I also learned the importance of expressing love to the dying. When I got home that evening, I prayed for Paul and his family. Paul died that next day. I was humbled with gratitude to assist him on his journey home. Nursing is a spiritual service; the care of the soul can never be separated from the care of the body.

Sometimes while walking down the hallway of the oncology unit, I intuitively know that this place is a waiting room between heaven and earth—and when your name is called, you go to your eternal home. When I met Patricia, she was on the oncology floor. Her doctor asked me to offer her holistic therapies, which at that time she was only minimally interested in. She enjoyed the guided imagery; she said it helped her to relax. As Patricia became more ill with end-stage colon cancer, she became more open to spiritual therapies. During my daily visits with her, she expressed a desire for the comfort of prayer and always wanted to hold my hand when we prayed. She said, "Thank you, God, for my life—and please help my family when I leave them." One day, we both experienced a strong presence of God that had settled over her, and she prayed—thanking him for her life and family. Many times her son and husband would join us in prayer at her bedside. One late morning, I entered her room to find her son very excited. He said, "I can't believe what happened this morning. My mother sat up in bed, appeared to be looking at someone, and said, 'Yes, Jesus, I am ready to go with you now.' Then she turned slightly and starting talking to my grandmother." When I took Patricia's hand that day I knew she had already started to take her journey home, but she wasn't going alone.

The supervisor of 2 West asked me to calm a patient down after he came very close to punching a nurse. While walking to the unit, I asked God to come and bring intervention for this troubled, agitated soul. Since I was trained in pastoral care, I introduced myself as both a nurse and a pastoral care agent. Intuitively, I knew to remain silent as Bob ranted and raved about the nurse and the delay of the doctor. The real issue, however, was that Bob had just received a poor diagnosis. The routine chest X-ray had revealed a tumor on his lung. I kept a calm, quiet composure and began to experience the presence of God flowing through me. I could feel a flow of energy coming out of my eyes. It was powerful, and it changed the entire atmosphere of the room. The vibration was ethereal. Bob's conversation went to a deeper level, and he began to share some regrets about his life. I realized I was taking on the role of an intercessor as Bob was confessing his past failures. His whole countenance changed when he said, "You know, I really do believe there is a God—I can see him in your eyes." When I left Bob's room that day, I was in awe of the magnitude of God's love for us.

> *There are no moments in our lives which are not holy, for God*
> *is present in every moment.*—Pierre de Caussade (1981)

Today we are experiencing a resurgence of spirituality in health care, which is a universal human/divine phenomenon. Using practices related to spiritual care, including prayer as a spiritual intervention, may restore wholeness and preserve the integrity of the patient. Because holistic nursing involves the spirituality of both nurse and patient, it is transformational for both.

There is much hope for the future of nursing. As its soul becomes transformed, health care and all society for that matter will experience a rebirth. As we choose life in the spirit over soul life, we will experience an increase of illumination (understanding) and revelation knowledge of the divine Creator. When the soul is renewed, it becomes more compatible with the spiritual dimension and its awareness of the divine increases. We discover we have a changed heart and a generous spirit with benevolent regard for humanity. As we understand exponentially that God treasures every individual soul with an infinite, measureless, and enduring love, then we will know what it means to have fellowship with God and "walk in the spirit." This is God's eternal purpose for us. God, who created us, guides us and still speaks to us today.

Travelers cannot reach new territory if they do not take new and unknown roads and abandon the familiar ones. John of the Cross spoke of his own journey to God as being a dark night of the soul. He said the only light of understanding he had was the flame of desire that burned in his heart. These words should inspire us. Desiring to transform your soul will propel you on the path to finding its fulfillment. As your mind becomes renewed, you will find your true self is spirit. It is only the flame of desire that will initiate the process of metamorphosis. As you shed the narrow confines, the cocoon of natural thought processes, you will discover that you have wings to fly. When your soul is transformed, you will see God, and you will reflect his beauty.

> *And this is the way to eternal life . . . to know you.*—John 17:3

A Closing Prayer

Most gracious and loving heavenly Father, may the transforming power of your resurrection transform all who read this. And may the mystery of communion, the breaking of bread, be theirs; may they share in this mystery by their spiritual eyes opening to behold you, and in beholding you, may they be changed into your image, which is their true identity and their true fulfillment. Amen.

AFTERWORD

This book is an invitation to recognize the rich heritage and power of nursing, to connect with the human spirit, and to recommence the profession to its true essence. Reading through the pages of the book may have created a myriad of emotions, questions, and insights; for some of you it could have been a validation of your beliefs and experiences, for others the concepts may be novel and need more study and reflection, and there may be many of you who find the abstract concepts or experiences  uncomfortable, questionable, and in need of evidence that you can substantiate.

The purpose here is to explore the perspectives described in the previous chapters through the lens of the three nurse leaders quoted in the book; Florence Nightingale, Martha Rogers, and Jean Watson.

In Florence Nightingale's biography, her choice of nursing as a means for serving humanity is attributed to hearing the call from God to serve mankind. Martha Rogers epitomized nursing as a "magnificent epic of service to mankind" (Rogers, 1970, P. ix). Jean Watson's theory of Human Caring Science is also consistent with nursing serving people to promote health and healing. Clearly, the theme of nursing as a service to mankind resonates from all three leaders.

Nightingale's approach was not just about caring for the sick through medical treatments, she believed in the concepts of health and wellness and worked hard to improve conditions and create an environment that would foster health and healing. Through the pages of history, we see her as a visionary, scholar, scientist, statistician, educator, authentic leader, advocate, activist, and reformer. Today, these roles are essential for sustaining and advancing the profession and we recognize the need to retrace our steps and move away from just providing episodic care to promoting health and wellness to the populations under our care.

Rogers stipulates that "the concern of nursing is with man in his entirety, his wholeness" (Rogers, 1970, p.3). This requires acknowledging totality of body, mind, and spirit. While we need to understand these attributes, we need to recognize that human existence is more than just the sum of the three. Rogers' assumption educates us; "Man is a unified whole possessing his own integrity and manifesting characteristics that are more than and different from the sum of its parts" (Rogers, 1970, p.47). Although initially she used the word 'man' to mean human beings, in her later work she changed it to 'unitary human being' to more completely represent the unique characteristics of human beings as an irreducible, indivisible, pandimensional energy field (Rogers, 1990).

With the progress of science and technology we have grown in our knowledge of treating the biophysical aspects of man while the principles of psychiatry and psychology enables us to treat mental illnesses and care for the emotional needs of man. As our knowledge advances, we are more secure and skilled in the areas of body and mind. Although the recognition of the need for honoring human spirituality is growing, the current level of abstraction about spirituality creates ambiguity.

The contradictions stem from multiple factors and start with the definition and meaning ascribed to spirituality. It is held as synonymous to religion by many and meeting the spiritual needs of a patient is often limited to providing the services of the priest, rabbi or their equivalent in different religions. The words soul and spirit are interchanged by some to mean the same thing and other viewpoints differentiate the two and consider the human spirit as the human essence that is connected to the divine while the soul is envisioned as being made up of the human intellect and emotions. Jean Watson (2012) uses the concept of the soul to mean the inner self, spirit, or essence of the person that is connected to a higher source of infinity. In summary, to date, there is no one conclusive definition.

While the above precepts may be endorsed and accepted by many as doctrines of theology, developing spiritual interventions and implications for nursing require another step. Science regards validation as a prerequisite for accepting developing concepts and scientific inquiry requires authentication directly or indirectly (use of instruments) through our five senses. If we had to learn from our history, the germ theory of diseases could only be substantiated after invention of the microscope. So, is it possible that the future will unveil the methods or instruments to accelerate our knowledge of spirituality? Or, are the methods already here known to the special few engaging in their study waiting to be released into main stream?

Are we evolving from just using our five senses to ways of knowing that we have not developed or recognized yet? Watson (2012) affirms a global shift, an awakening of human consciousness and a new reality of our connection to all living things and she cautions the need for nursing to consider the worldview of science and life. She cautions us with the need to be open to various forms of inquiry and knowing. Nursing accepts human spirituality and has a growing body of literature related to the meaning of spirituality to spiritual care. Thus, nursing has set the stage for endless possibilities and understands the need to be open to evolve with the evolution of life itself.

The book has several references to visions and healing, and a vitreous substance transferring from the healer to the person being healed. The occurrences can be explained through Martha Rogers' concepts related to the Science of Unitary Human Being. Her definition of human beings and environment as dynamic energy fields and pan-dimensionality, defined as a non-linear domain without spatial or temporal attributes allows all possibilities. Developments in the field of Kirlian photography are worth exploring for evidence of energy fields and energy transfer.

Nightingale instituted a firm foundation for nursing; Martha Rogers established nursing as a basic science. Nursing's journey to establish its credibility required nursing to follow science and scientific inquiry and Watson reminds us that "science, scientific development and theory development are all related to art, the humanities, and philosophy" (Watson, 2012, p.1.).

Intimately dealing with human existence, disease and health, nursing is well positioned to discover and articulate the intricacies of being human and caring for humans. However, it will require the collaboration of the multiple roles in nursing; clinicians, theorists, researchers, educators, and administrators will need to unite and remain open to emerging knowledge and multiple ways of knowing to move from abstract concepts to practical applications of honoring human spirituality.

—Lily Thomas, Ph.D., RN, FAAN, is the Vice President for System Nursing Research at the North Shore – LIJ Health System.

BIBLIOGRAPHY

Aspen Reference Group. 2002. *Guided Imagery Book: Holistic Health Promotion and Complementary Therapies.* New York: Aspen.

Baker, William, and Michael O'Malley. 2008. *Leading with Kindness.* New York: AMACOM.

Boyd, Tracy. 2013. "Pillars of nursing: North Shore—LIJ's White works to foster art and science of profession." *nurse.com.* March.

Brother Lawrence. 1967. *The Practice of the Presence of God.* Revell.

Campbell, J. 1972. *Myths to Live By.* New York: Viking Press.

Chopra, Deepak. 2003. *The Spontaneous Fulfillment of Desire.* New York: Crown Publishing Group.

Clark, Glenn. 1924. *The Soul's Sincere Desire. Atlantic Monthly.*

Conner, Bobby. 2011. *Shepherd's Rod* XVII. Bullard, TX: Eagles View Ministries.

Davis, Paul Keith. 2007. *Angels That Gather.* Dove Company Publishing.

de Caussade, Jean-Pierre. 1981. *The Sacrament of the Present Moment,* English translation. Glasgow: William Collins Sons and Co. Ltd.

———. 2009. *The Sacrament of the Present Moment,* Reissue Edition. Translated by Kitty Muggeridge. HarperSanFrancisco.

de Chardin, T. (1967). *On Love.* New York: Harper & Row.

De Mille, Agnes. 1991. *Martha: The Life and Work of Martha Graham.* Random House.

Dickens, Charles. 1867. *A Tale of Two Cities*. New York: H. Wolff Book Co.

Dolan, J. A. *Nursing in Society: A Historical Perspective*, 15th ed. Philadelphia: Saunders, 1983.

Dossey, Barbara Montgomery. 2009. *Florence Nightingale: Mystic, Visionary, Healer*. F. A. Davis Company.

Dossey, B.M., Beck, D.M., Selanders. L.C., Alex Attewell, Editor (2005). *Florence Nightingale Today: Healing, Leadership Global Action*

Egan, Harvey D. 1998. *Karl Rahner: Mystic of Everyday Life*.

Emoto, Masaru. 2004. *The Hidden Messages in Water*. Hillsboro, OR: Beyond Words Publishing.

Fiorelli, Lewis S., ed. 1985. *The Sermons of Saint Frances De Sales on Prayer*. Rockford, IL: Tan Books and Publishers.

Foster, J. Richard. 2005. *Freedom of Simplicity*. Harper One Publishers

Greene, Brian. 1999. *The Elegant Universe: Superstrings, Hidden Dimensions, and the Quest for the Ultimate Theory*. New York: W. W. Norton & Company.

Hampson, Mary, ed. 1960. *The Complete Poems of Emily Dickinson*. Library of Congress, 14th edition.

Hicks, Mark. 2012. *Surprise the Union of Quantum Physics, Relativity, and the Bible*. Wine Press Publishing.

Jablonowski, Paul. 2006. *Sons to Glory*. Harvest, AL.

Johnson, Neville. 2010. *The Power of Words*, iPod Video. Academy of Light.

Keachie, Julia. 1992. "Gentle Persuasion." *Nursing Times* 88 (6).

Lake, John G. 1991. *Adventures in God*. Tulsa, OK: Harrison House.

———. 1999. *John G. Lake: The Complete Collection of His Life Teaching*. Tulsa, OK: Alburn Publishing.

Lewis, C. S. 1955. *The Chronicles of Narnia 6: The Magician's Nephew*. New York: HarperCollins.

Longfellow, Henry Wadsworth. 1857. "Santa Filomena." *The Atlantic Monthly* 1(1): 22–23.

Louchs, James F., and Andrew M. Stauffer. 2007. *Robert Browning's Poetry*, Norton Critical Edition.

Lucado, Max. 1999. *He Still Moves Stones.* Nashville, TN: Thomas Nelson.

Maher, Anthony. "A Night Nurse's Prayer," *The Catholic Nurse* 2:4 (1954): 30.

McDonald, Lynn, ed. 2002. *Florence Nightingale's Theology: Essays, Letters and Journal Notes.* Waterloo, ON, Canada: Wilfrid Laurier University Press.

Nightingale, Florence. 1859. *Notes on Nursing: What It Is and What It Is Not.* London: Scutari Press.

O'Brien, Mary Elizabeth. 1999. *Spirituality in Nursing: Standing on Holy Ground.* Sudbury, MA: Jones and Bartlett Publishers.

———. 2003. *Prayer in Nursing.* Jones and Bartlett Publishers.

Rogers, Martha. 1970. *An Introduction to the Theoretical Basis of Nursing.* Philadelphia: F.A. Davis Company

Rogers, Martha. 1989. *Nursing: The Science of Unitary Human Beings.* Thousand Oaks, CA: Sage.

———. 1990. *Visions of Rogers' Science-Based Nursing.* New York: National League for Nursing.

Rosenberg C. E. 1979. "Florence Nightingale on Contagion: The Hospital as Moral Universe." In *Healing and History: Essays for George Rosen.* New York: Watson Publishing.

Ross, L. 2006, "Spiritual care in nursing: An overview of the research to date." *Journal of Clinical Nursing* 15: 852–862.

Rothweiler, Ella L. 1937. *The Science and Art of Nursing.* Philadelphia: F. A. Davis Company.

"Stress Busting Smiles," *Psychological Sciences*, November 2012.

Swedenborg, Emanuel. 1966. *Heaven and Hell.* Boston: Swedenborg Printing Bureau.

Taylor, Wade E. 2007. *Unlocking the Mysteries of the Kingdom.* Capitol Heights, MD: Wade Taylor Publications.

Teilhard de Chardin, Pierre. 1959. *The Phenomenon of Man*. New York: Harper & Row Publishers.

The Publishing Program of American Nurses Association. 2005. *Florence Nightingale Today*. Silver Spring, Md. The Publishing Program of American Nurses Association.

Thompson, William J. "Nurse's Prayer at Graduation Exercises." *The Trained Nurse and Hospital Review* 103.7 (1939): 15.

Trudeau, Kevin. 2006. *Natural Cures "They" Don't Want You to Know About*. Birmingham, AL: Alliance Publishing Group.

Van Koevering, David. 2007. *Keys to Taking Your Quantum Leap*. Elsewhere Research.

Watson, Jean. 2012. *Human Caring Science: A Theory of Nursing (Second Edition)*. Sudbury, MA: Jones and Bartlett Learning.

Watson, Jean. 1999. *Nursing: Human Science and Human Care: A Theory of Nursing*. Sudbury, MA: Jones and Bartlett Publishers.

Watson, Jean. 2011.Creating A Caring Science Curriculum. Springer Publishing Co.,LLC

Hodge, 2001, Joseph, 1988; Standard, Sandhu, and Painter, 2000

Watson, Jean. 1999. *Postmodern Nursing and Beyond*. New York: Churchill Livingstone.

Widerquist, J. G. 1992. "The spirituality of Florence Nightingale." Nurs Res. 4149-55.55 (PubMed).

Williamson, Marianne. 1992. *A Return to Love: Reflections on the Principles of a Course in Miracles*. HarperCollins Publishers.

Yonggi Cho, David. 1979. *The Fourth Dimension: Discovering a New World of Answered Prayer*. Alachua, FL: Bridge-Logos Publishers.

Zander, Rosamund Stone, and Benjamin Zander. 2002. *The Art of Possibility*. New York: Penguin Books.

OTHER SOURCES

http://www.monisticidealism.wordpress.com. September 2007.

http://www.pbs.org/faithandreason/theogloss/logos-body.html.

http://www.goodvibeblog.com/what-quiff-are-you-poppin/ (Jeannette Maw) blog, September 29, 2010.

http://en.wikipedia.org/wiki/Michael J. Dowling

http://www.webmd.com/balance/stress-management/tc/ guided-imagery-topic-overview.

http://www.nasa.gov/centers/marshall/news/news/ releases/2003/03-152.html.

http://www.gsfc.nasa/scienceques2003/20031003.htm-headlinesy 2003/09sep-blackholesounds.htm.

National Cancer Institute, http://www.cancer.gov/can-cerrtopics/ pdq/treatment/prostate/Patient/page4.

Jeannette Maw's *Good Vibe* blog,

goodvibeblog.com/what-quiff-are-you-poppin/.

http://en.wikipedia.org/wiki/BrotherLawrence.

www.heartlight.org/wjd/matthew/1121-wjd.html.

http/www.ncbi.nih.gov/pmc/articles/PMC2563330.

http://online.wsj.com/articles/SB10001424127887323699704578326363601444362.html.

University College Cork, Ireland. http//www.ucc,ie/en/

www.goodreads.com/quotes/tag/ablert-einstein)

OPEN HEAVEN

Book Cover: Open Heaven

The cover of this book was created out of an incredibly awesome experience I had several years ago. One evening as I laid down to sleep I found myself moving out of my body and going upward out of my room to what next appeared to be the universe. While gliding upward I immediately saw a wide staircase to my right and I was gliding over them. I could see bright white cloud like formations that appeared all around me, I was going through them with graceful ease. As I continued to glide upward through the clouds a door appeared. When I looked at the door it suddenly opened. A bright blindly penetrating light came bursting through the door and though it hurt my eyes to keep looking at its' brightness, I couldn't take my eyes off the awesome scene. Immediately, without warning I heard what I thought was an angel; because he spoke with great authority... *'Come up here, and I will show you what is to come'*. I was speechless, and in awe of the wonder of it all. Moments later I felt myself moving slowly downward, I was gliding back into my bed... I said, *'you will never ever forget this'*.

The book cover came out of what some may call a visitation from God. After sharing my heavenly experience with artist, Janice Van Chorte, she agreed to paint it and titled it 'Open Heaven.' There is a very clear message in it. I believe an invitation is being offered to humanity at this prophetic time in history. It invites us to come up higher and be transformed into our spiritual heritage. As this present age comes to a close, the creator is graciously extending an invitation to us to participate in His kingdom reign that is soon to come on the earth.